Praise for *Psalms for Black Lives*

Avery*Sunshine, BET Award nominee and Billboard chart-topping artist

"In this introspective daily study of the book of Psalms, Pastors Gabby and Andrew successfully address the concerns of our people, help us unpack our feelings around injustices, give voice to the shared feelings of the collective and challenge us to be bold in envisioning life, and our lives, differently. This is the liberating Bible study that I've longed for and love to share."

Risë Nelson, Director of Diversity, Equity and Inclusion at Yale University Library

"Pastors Gabby and Andrew have made this offering from and of love as a reminder of who you and *we* are. It is an invitation to renew your faith in God *and* in the power of our community. It is a confirmation of God's plan for each of us and of God's promise to be with us in our challenges and our victories. With and through this offering, may you find peace, safety, inspiration, courage, joy, and faith!"

D1736868

PSALMS
for
BLACK
LIVES

REFLECTIONS *for the*
WORK *of* LIBERATION

GABBY CUDJOE-WILKES AND ANDREW WILKES

UPPER
ROOM BOOKS®
NASHVILLE

This book is inspired by—and we pray, a fitting tribute to—the countless individuals, organizers, collectives, and assemblies fighting, struggling, and planning for the liberation of Black lives, which is a precondition for the liberation for humanity.

We dedicate this book to the Black lives and lineage that came before us—the ones who loved us, raised us, and championed us on toward good works from birth—the Burnetts, the Longs, the Wilkes, the Cudjoes, and the Waters.

We dedicate this also to the Black church traditions that formed us: Zion Hill Baptist Church, Atlanta, Georgia, The Greater Allen A.M.E. Cathedral of New York, and The Trinity United Church of Christ, Chicago, Illinois. We give special thanks to the senior pastors of those congregations, our mentors: Reverend Doctors Parker, Flake, McCollins Flake, and Moss III.

We honor the founding members of the congregation we launched, who believed in the vision and have given us the double honor of allowing us to be their pastors at The Double Love Experience Church in Brooklyn, New York. We also honor our denominational home, The Progressive National Baptist Convention.

Of warm, special note, we dedicate this book to our home by the sea, Hampton University, our personal birthplace of love and ministry. It was on that campus on April 17, 2005, that we began our journey of love, in a sea of Black lives, with bright dreams and big hopes for our future.

CONTENTS

PART III: PRACTICING PSALMS FOR BLACK LIVES: A COMMUNITY AND CONGREGATIONAL STUDY GUIDE

FOREWORD

*"The poet invents heroic moments where
the pale Black ancestor stands up on behalf
of the race." —Elizabeth Alexander*

Poets, psalmists, and the griot are children of the same womb, nurtured by waters sweetened with hope, yet sour with the blues. Elizabeth Alexander is right. The poet is an orchestrator of worlds, part blues, a dash of hope, a taste of imminence, with enough transcendence to cause the imagination to call the names of Octavia Butler, Amos, bell hooks, and Martin Luther King, Jr. in the same breath.

This is the power of poetry. It is an art form that bears witness with words designed to deconstruct poisonous assumptions. The psalmists of the Hebraic community dared such a feat, to crush the myths that infected the minds of people living in exile and replace them with the story of a God beyond human categorization but present in human affairs. The Psalms were not solely songs of praise but poetry of triumph, tragedy, frustration, existential crisis, sorrow, heartbreak, joy, and at times, rage.

*"How can we sing the songs of the LORD while
in a foreign land?" —Psalm 137:4 (NIV)*

The psalmists center the condition of exile, the pain of exclusion, and the yearning of nationhood as a preeminent priority for the people of Israel, a people marginalized by an empire they live within but are not full citizens of. It is the eternal struggle of the Jewish exile, for they are people still haunted by a history built upon a racial mythos created by people who seek to exploit their labor. The poet, the psalmist, and the griot are all one in these poetic battles constructed by writers and lovers of Israel.

It is the duty of the psalmist to center the world of a person in exile who lives behind the veil, who is caught between two worlds as the subject of God's concern and action. The psalmist may mention Babylon, but the purpose of the poetry is not to uplift the empire. These words give voice to those carried off by unrepentant empires, and allow us to understand their lives—their Black lives—in the wider economy of God's creation.

It is within this rhythm that the prophetic, pastoral couple, Gabby Cudjoe-Wilkes and Andrew Wilkes, pen this book of poetic and prophetic devotions that dare to center the lives of Black people caught in exile and entanglement with the American project.

The Wilkes are children of what scholars call "Black religiosity." This catch-all term is more than religious ritual, and conveys a cultural and spiritual heritage that draws from West Africa, Southern Black sensibilities, and Afro-Atlantic tradition. A more precise term might be "creolization," but even this term does not capture the holistic nature of the Wilkes' spiritual heritage. While their upbringing is Southern, their education and love story was written on the campus of Hampton University where the colliding worlds of Black tradition and educational sensibilities coalesce to create a thoughtful and radicalized interpretation of what it means to be faithful, Black, and a believer.

This book you hold in your hand is more than a devotional. It is an amalgamation of ancient words written by ancestors whose names have been lost, yet reclaimed through the spiritual practice of the Wilkes family. The words on these pages were written by Gabby and Andrew Wilkes, but the editors of this volume have names such as Emmitt, Goodman, Breonna, Henry, George, Eric, Dawn, Trayvon, Philando, and many others.

May the work of this brilliant couple bless you as they have blessed the lives of countless people across this nation. May you be blessed by the *Psalms for Black Lives*.

Rev. Dr. Otis Moss III, Senior Pastor
Trinity United Church of Christ, Chicago, IL

INTRODUCTION

In the summer of 2020, America burned, often literally, with a passion for racial justice and righteous indignation over the murder of Black lives, among them George Floyd, Breonna Taylor, and Tony McDade. At the Double Love Experience Church, the church we founded and launched in Brooklyn, New York, we called for a churchwide fast. For eight days, we prayed together, took part in civic action together, *and* read Psalms together. These eight days led to six months of Wednesday prayer sessions where we read and reflected on the Psalms as a community. In beautiful ways, some expected, many unforeseen, God encouraged our hearts during a difficult moment in America, a land where democracy, after all these years, is still struggling to be born.

The Psalms are rediscovered with fresh eyes by every generation. They speak across differences in cultures, social contexts, and even centuries. The Psalms are beloved for their emotional rawness, their urge toward justice, and their blunt candor about the coarse edges of a life spent walking with God.

While composing devotionals about the Psalms for our Double Love congregation, we recognized that the spiritual and social concerns of our congregation were shared by many outside of our immediate community as well. People across the globe, especially those across the African diaspora, found themselves navigating dual pandemics, the global pandemic of COVID-19 and the domestic pandemic of Black bodies being killed in the streets by those sworn to protect them. People of faith around the world were in desperate need of spiritual resources to keep them going. We realized that the work we were doing at our church might be for an audience larger than just our congregation. People were struggling, and the Psalms were the perfect place to begin looking for help.

As we engaged with the Psalms, our research, our prayers, and our vocation reinforced our belief about the importance of the Psalms as a contemplative resource for those doing the holy, demanding work of pursuing justice, undoing structural racism, and building a society that truly values Black lives.

We hope that after making your way through this devotional, you will be able to dream afresh about the possibilities of seeing justice come alive in our time. Whether you are reading this book with your congregation, your community, your class, or just your own thoughts, our prayer is that this work will help you develop a *justice imagination* that can speak a comprehensive, hands-on word of spirituality and social transformation into this racist, economically unequal, yet deeply hungry and hopeful moment.

A justice imagination is resistance at work. In a time period when folks laugh at us for believing justice is possible, those with a justice imagination find it within their hearts to imagine anyhow. That is our hope for you, that you might come away from this devotional with a desire to imagine a better world despite the pain of the moment. Despite the headlines, imagine anyhow. Despite the verdicts, imagine anyhow. We speak the power and possibility of a justice imagination over you and your family. You can dream afresh. All is not lost. There's hope awaiting you.

As you build your justice imagination, we will highlight the ways that the Psalms speak to four different actions we undertake in the work of liberation. We celebrate together, we lament together, we envision together, and we are emboldened together.

The work of celebration is fundamental to fostering and embodying a justice imagination. Just as the book of Genesis records God pausing to declare that God's creation was good each day, our work of redesigning systems of harm for more just outcomes deserves notice, applause, and affirmation. We invite you to pause and celebrate both large and small steps toward justice. Everything from staffing a table to registering voters to organizing a protest to helping to introduce legislation deserves celebration. All of it matters, all of it, in the spirit of the Psalms, is an occasion to celebrate the God of love and justice, whose holy presence makes the work of our hands possible.

Alongside celebration, the Psalms invite us to lament together. Lament is a recurring theme of the Psalms and a necessary dimension of spiritual and emotional health. Through lament, we grieve our losses, honor our feelings, and invite God into the messiness of our lives as they truly are rather than how we would prefer them to be. When Nehemiah mobilized his community to rebuild the shattered walls of Jerusalem, he began with lament. Tears and anguish for all the pain the people had endured marked the start of that great undertaking. Inspired by that example, let us make space for our tears and, in the process, make way for a justice imagination that can rebuild what is ruptured in our communities.

The Psalms also push us to envision the world in new ways. There are times when we need to visualize the ways

God can work in our lives. If we aren't careful, the wear and tear of striving for justice can keep us from seeing anything new. We need the grace of God to help us envision new possibilities in our lives. We need God to help us illuminate our own justice imagination. The Psalms call us to envision the world the way that God sees it. No more false binaries. No more fatalistic ways of being. We choose to envision great things. We choose to see what God sees.

The Psalms also embolden our faith. Life can be trying at times, but let us endeavor to be more bold. We have the right to bring our concerns *boldly* to the throne of grace. We have the right to *boldly* claim the promises of God, both for ourselves and for our people. We have the right to *boldly* ask God for what we need. We must *boldly* believe that change is possible!

For each of the psalms selected over the next thirty days, you'll find not only a reflection about how the psalm connects to the work of liberation and justice that we are undertaking together, but also a devotional invitation that seeks to help you meditate further on the message and meaning behind the text. Furthermore, to help you sort out how each psalm speaks to the actions of celebration, lament, envisioning, and emboldening, we've included daily questions that you can use either as an individual or as a small group to push deeper and see how each psalm can truly connect with your work, your life, and your community.

You might need to revisit some of these psalms more than once before your justice imagination is ignited. Do not let that discourage you. Read each psalm, each reflection, and each devotional as many times as you must. Read them out of order if you need to. Take your time with each question. Let God speak to you and through you. Use this devotional as your guide for building and renewing your capacity to imagine.

We are at a critical juncture for Black people across the diaspora. It may yet become a turning point of our nation's history. May we pause to encounter the Psalms as a sacred word for *and* to Black lives.

In faith, hope, and love,
Pastor Gabby and Pastor Andrew

Defiant Confidence

Psalm 27

The LORD is my light and my salvation;
    whom shall I fear?
The LORD is the stronghold of my life;
    of whom shall I be afraid?

When evildoers assail me
    to devour my flesh—
my adversaries and foes—
    they shall stumble and fall.

Though an army encamp against me,
    my heart shall not fear;
though war rise up against me,
    yet I will be confident.

One thing I asked of the LORD,
    that will I seek after:
to live in the house of the LORD
    all the days of my life,
to behold the beauty of the LORD,
    and to inquire in his temple.

For he will hide me in his shelter
    in the day of trouble;
he will conceal me under the cover of his tent;
    he will set me high on a rock.

Now my head is lifted up
    above my enemies all around me,
and I will offer in his tent
    sacrifices with shouts of joy;
I will sing and make melody to the LORD.

Hear, O LORD, when I cry aloud,
    be gracious to me and answer me!
"Come," my heart says, "seek his face!"
    Your face, LORD, do I seek.
    Do not hide your face from me.

Do not turn your servant away in anger,
    you who have been my help.
Do not cast me off, do not forsake me,
    O God of my salvation!
If my father and mother forsake me,
    the LORD will take me up.

Teach me your way, O LORD,
    and lead me on a level path
    because of my enemies.
Do not give me up to the will of my adversaries,
    for false witnesses have risen against me,
    and they are breathing out violence.

I believe that I shall see the goodness of the LORD
    in the land of the living.

Wait for the LORD;
    be strong, and let your heart take courage;
    wait for the LORD!

Reflection

It can be a struggle to believe that anything is enough to overcome our fear, even God, our light and our salvation. This psalm invites us to wonder what life could look like if fear ceased to dominate.

Psalm 27 encourages us to live boldly, courageously, and powerfully. Our faith doesn't remove us from intimidating situations, and this psalm acknowledges that reality in the first two verses, envisioning a terrifying scenario where "evildoers assail me to devour my flesh" and "war rise up against me." Having faith does not mean avoiding reality. Faith, instead, addresses intimidating circumstances with defiant confidence in God. After describing a host of imposing realities, the psalmist pushes back in verse 3, saying, "Yet I will be confident."

The defiant confidence of the psalmist is attainable for each of us. To the full extent of your ability, you can push back, with God-soaked conviction, against opposition in your life. Yes, social distancing can take a toll. Yes, screen fatigue is real. Yes, shouldering long hours at work—or even looking for work in the first place—can be taxing. But, like the psalmist, we can be defiantly confident. God is our shelter and our hiding place (v. 5). We overcome fear by approaching every situation as an opportunity to lean on God as our light who brings direction, our salvation who brings us safety, and our stronghold who protects us when we're vulnerable (v. 1).

With defiant confidence, we charge you to wait on the Lord today (v. 14). "Be strong and let your heart take courage," for together we will see the goodness of God in the land of the living (v. 14).

Devotional

Cultivating a justice imagination requires defiant confidence. Defiant confidence confronts intimidating circumstances. It replaces our fears about what might go wrong with the convictions of what might go right if we take courageous action.

Breathe in, then exhale deeply. As you breathe, ask yourself what defiant confidence means for you. After several breaths, write down one or two sentences about what it would look like for you to walk unapologetically in the knowledge that God is your light and salvation.

Questions for the Day

- Building a justice imagination requires courage. How might we embody the defiant confidence of the psalmist?
- What does it look like to lament the moments when we could have exercised defiant confidence but ultimately did not?
- Where is the celebration in this psalm? What gives you hope? What makes you shout?

Who Are the Wicked?

Psalm 1:1-6

Happy are those
    who do not follow the advice of the wicked,
or take the path that sinners tread,
    or sit in the seat of scoffers;
but their delight is in the law of the LORD,
    and on his law they meditate day and night.
They are like trees
    planted by streams of water,
which yield their fruit in its season,
    and their leaves do not wither.
In all that they do, they prosper.

The wicked are not so,
    but are like chaff that the wind drives away.
Therefore the wicked will not stand in the judgment,
    nor sinners in the congregation of the righteous;
for the LORD watches over the way of the righteous,
    but the way of the wicked will perish.

Reflection

If we're not careful with this psalm, it can cause us to think more highly of ourselves than we should. The psalmist advises us not to keep company with the wicked, or scoffers, or those who take the path of sinners (v. 1). While this is good advice, it leaves us with an important question: Who are the wicked?

In truth, each of us has the capacity to be wicked. Each of us has the capacity to turn on those we love, to seek what we desire regardless of how it affects others. The psalmist says that the antidote for wickedness is to delight in the law of the Lord *and* meditate on the law day and night (v. 2). Don't miss that. The two work together. It is both the ability to delight in God's ways and the discipline of meditating on God's law that helps us avoid wickedness.

When you undertake both these actions together, you will become so rooted in your faith that even when you might desire to be wicked, you will have built up defenses to fight off that desire. *This* is why you should not keep company with the wicked. It takes work to keep yourself from giving in to wickedness. It takes preparation and focus. Keeping close company with those who aren't committed to beating back wickedness is a sure way to lower your defenses and cause your own foot to slip.

This does not mean that you should socialize only with people who act like you. It does mean, however, that you should not expect wise counsel from those who are not committed to beating back wickedness. That will not yield good fruit in your life.

As we meditate on God's word today, we charge you to find pleasure and delight in what God has said over your life.

When your spirit is consumed with the Word of the Lord, you can respond to life's challenges with an arsenal of biblical wisdom. We believe God is making you wiser day by day. The psalmist says that those who delight in the Lord and meditate on the scriptures will yield fruit in season. Their leaves will not wither and the work of their hand will prosper (v. 3). This means you. You are the person the psalmist is describing. What a promise! What a gift!

Devotional

Action gets all the attention, but the spiritual discipline of silence is essential to enrich a justice imagination. Analyzing the root causes of injustice and taking action to redress those causes won't sustain us on their own. We also need something beyond words. Silence calls us to wordless communion with the Holy One—and with ourselves. It gives us space to examine ourselves. Have I been wicked in my own deeds? Am I complicit? Am I contributing more to the problem than the solution? This communion allows our justice imagination to grow and flourish, and that imagination inspires us to action.

Take a few minutes to sit in silence. Remain as still as you can. Breathe in and out. As you stay silent, turn the words of this psalm into an affirmation: "I am like a tree, planted by streams of water, bearing fruit in its season."

Questions for the Day

- What would happen if we embraced silence as a pathway into being "like a tree, planted by streams of water, bearing fruit in its season"? How would this change the way we approach prayer? How would it change the way we approach life's challenges?

- How does silence and the use of language contrast with the scoffing and "advice of the wicked" in this passage? Have you ever withheld words when a time to speak was at hand? Conversely, recall a time where your words flooded a conversation, perhaps in the form of scoffing cautioned against in this passage, and prevented others from participating. How did your use of language, including a possible decision not to speak, affect each of these situations?

Safe

Psalm 91

You who live in the shelter of the Most High,
    who abide in the shadow of the Almighty,
will say to the LORD, "My refuge and my fortress;
    my God, in whom I trust."
For he will deliver you from the snare of the fowler
    and from the deadly pestilence;
he will cover you with his pinions,
    and under his wings you will find refuge;
his faithfulness is a shield and buckler.
You will not fear the terror of the night,
    or the arrow that flies by day,
or the pestilence that stalks in darkness,
    or the destruction that wastes at noonday.

A thousand may fall at your side,
    ten thousand at your right hand,
    but it will not come near you.
You will only look with your eyes
    and see the punishment of the wicked.

Because you have made the LORD your refuge,
    the Most High your dwelling place,

no evil shall befall you,
    no scourge come near your tent.

For he will command his angels concerning you
    to guard you in all your ways.
On their hands they will bear you up,
    so that you will not dash your foot against a stone.
You will tread on the lion and the adder,
    the young lion and the serpent you will trample under
    foot.

Those who love me, I will deliver;
    I will protect those who know my name.
When they call to me, I will answer them;
    I will be with them in trouble,
    I will rescue them and honor them.
With long life I will satisfy them,
    and show them my salvation.

Reflection

When we were children, many of us played the game hide
and seek. When playing that game, nothing feels quite as
empowering as locating a perfect hiding place where no one
can find you. When you consider the special hideouts that we
had as young people—our favorite parks, treehouses, pools,
community centers, basketball courts—we all had places that
made us feel safe. Those spaces were necessary for our for-
mation, for our self-confidence, and for our livelihood. But
as we grow older, the world begins to feel bigger. Our lives
expand to the point that having a sanctuary like that, a safe

little hideout, now seems foolish. The older we get, the more exposed we feel.

Yet Psalm 91 offers us the comforting message that God can be our hiding place. Spending time with God every day can actually be that special safe place, that sanctuary. We may no longer be children, *but we are still children of God.*

When you create space in your life for God to dwell, you create your own personal sanctuary. Everyone deserves a safe place. Everyone deserves a place to express themselves without limitation. Your time with God is just that.

When you rest safely in the presence of God, God promises to protect you and fight your battles. Today, we charge you to find sanctuary in your time with God. We encourage you to let down your guard. You can trust God. In your time alone with God, you can be your true self.

Devotional

St. Teresa of Avila, an iconic Christian mystic, once called the heart an "interior castle." Each of our hearts holds a spiritual fortress of renewal, a place where prayer and pushing for social change connect and reinforce one another.

With this in mind, use the following prayer to commune with the Lord:

> Lord, thank you for being our hiding place. You are our trauma-free zone. In your presence, there is safety, joy, and restoration for everyone. On this day, be serenity within my struggle, and be laughter amid my work for liberation.

Questions for the Day

- Describe what it would feel like to pray from within a spiritual fortress of renewal. Why would this kind of fortification be necessary to nurture a justice imagination?
- The psalmist talks about abiding in the shadow of the Almighty. In the brush harbors of the antebellum, pre-Civil War South, Black Christians communed with the Divine, abiding in God's presence. What are your experiences of abiding—being held and accompanied—near God?

Rejoice

Psalm 34 (KJV)

I will bless the LORD at all times: his praise shall continually
be in my mouth.

My soul shall make her boast in the LORD: the humble shall
hear thereof, and be glad.

O magnify the LORD with me, and let us exalt his name
together.

I sought the LORD, and he heard me, and delivered me from
all my fears.

They looked unto him, and were lightened: and their faces
were not ashamed.

This poor man cried, and the LORD heard him, and saved
him out of all his troubles.

The angel of the LORD encampeth round about them that
fear him, and delivereth them.

O taste and see that the LORD is good: blessed is the man
that trusteth in him.

O fear the LORD, ye his saints: for there is no want to them
that fear him.

The young lions do lack, and suffer hunger: but they that
seek the LORD shall not want any good thing.

Come, ye children, hearken unto me: I will teach you the
    fear of the Lord.
What man is he that desireth life, and loveth many days,
    that he may see good?
Keep thy tongue from evil, and thy lips from speaking guile.
Depart from evil, and do good; seek peace, and pursue it.
The eyes of the Lord are upon the righteous, and his ears
    are open unto their cry.
The face of the Lord is against them that do evil, to cut off
    the remembrance of them from the earth.
The righteous cry, and the Lord heareth, and delivereth
    them out of all their troubles.
The Lord is nigh unto them that are of a broken heart; and
    saveth such as be of a contrite spirit.
Many are the afflictions of the righteous: but the Lord
    delivereth him out of them all.
He keepeth all his bones: not one of them is broken.
Evil shall slay the wicked: and they that hate the righteous
    shall be desolate.
The Lord redeemeth the soul of his servants: and none of
    them that trust in him shall be desolate.

Reflection

Praise is the native tongue of the believer. The psalmist
expresses this beautifully saying, "I will bless the Lord at
all times: his praise shall continually be in my mouth." This
commitment to praise *at all times* also means honoring God
in all situations, including the most troubling ones. This is an
important challenge for Christians, but praising God, always
and everywhere, can also be an intimidating charge. What

kind of perspective informs this practice of praise? What sort of attitude motivates the desire to praise God, not just in pleasant and pain-free times, but rather, all times?

The psalmist supplies an answer in verse four, "I sought the LORD, and he heard me, and delivered me from all my fears." Remembering how God answers our prayers and delivers us from our fears provides us a powerful reason to praise God even when things aren't going well. Take a few minutes to think about it. Recall a time when God answered your prayers or helped you overcome your fears. The psalmist argues, wisely, that these moments are the basis for our ongoing practice of praising God. Remembering these moments helps us make a habit of orienting ourselves toward God.

We find more reasons to praise God later in the psalm, particularly in verse eight. There, the psalmist memorably exclaims, "O taste and see that the LORD is good: blessed is the man that trusteth in him." Our praise flows from a joyous, firsthand experience of God's goodness. God's goodness wakes us up each day. God's goodness provides air to breathe and lungs to fill. God's goodness supplies food to savor and shelter to protect.

Why praise God at all times? Because the steadfast nature of our faithful God never changes. To use an enduring refrain of worship in the Black church, God is good all the time, and all the time, God is good.

Devotional

To riff on the African theologian St. Augustine, who is it that we praise when we praise God? The God of justice, who sides with the marginalized and downtrodden, is the God we exalt.

A justice imagination flows from worship that reserves adoration for a God of mercy, faithfulness, and equality.

In order to offer perpetual praise, it must also be personal praise. Consider your life for a moment. Which relationships, experiences, and memories spark a desire for you to praise God? Name at least three reasons to give thanks to a just, merciful God.

Questions for the Day

- Is there something God has done in your life that you've taken for granted? Make a list of the moments in your life where God showed up that you have somehow allowed yourself to ignore. Practice giving God praise for these moments today.
- In some Black churches, there is a "sick and shut-in list." This list traditionally includes members of the community who are, as the name implies, ill, homebound, or grappling with a health condition. Create a sick and shut-in list of your own that consists of at least two or three individuals. Pray for them regularly this week.
- What does it look like to include everyone in the community in our praise? How do we include those who are unable to join us in the worship of the community? What does it look like to help one another praise God in any situation?

Don't Forget!

Psalm 103

Bless the LORD, O my soul,
    and all that is within me,
      bless his holy name.
Bless the LORD, O my soul,
    and do not forget all his benefits—
who forgives all your iniquity,
    who heals all your diseases,
who redeems your life from the Pit,
    who crowns you with steadfast love and mercy,
who satisfies you with good as long as you live
    so that your youth is renewed like the eagle's.

The LORD works vindication
    and justice for all who are oppressed.
He made known his ways to Moses,
    his acts to the people of Israel.
The LORD is merciful and gracious,
    slow to anger and abounding in steadfast love.
He will not always accuse,
    nor will he keep his anger forever.
He does not deal with us according to our sins,
    nor repay us according to our iniquities.

For as the heavens are high above the earth,
    so great is his steadfast love toward those who fear him;
as far as the east is from the west,
    so far he removes our transgressions from us.
As a father has compassion for his children,
    so the LORD has compassion for those who fear him.
For he knows how we were made;
    he remembers that we are dust.

As for mortals, their days are like grass;
    they flourish like a flower of the field;
for the wind passes over it, and it is gone,
    and its place knows it no more.
But the steadfast love of the LORD is from everlasting to
    everlasting
    on those who fear him,
    and his righteousness to children's children,
to those who keep his covenant
    and remember to do his commandments.

The LORD has established his throne in the heavens,
    and his kingdom rules over all.
Bless the LORD, O you his angels,
    you mighty ones who do his bidding,
    obedient to his spoken word.
Bless the LORD, all his hosts,
    his ministers that do his will.
Bless the LORD, all his works,
    in all places of his dominion.
Bless the LORD, O my soul.

Reflection

For those of us who grew up in church, we've likely heard ministers say the words, "I will bless the Lord at all times . . .," but what it means to bless the Lord is not immediately clear. If you've been in church awhile, you've likely become accustomed to that language, but, if we're honest, language like this is frequently used, yet rarely explained.

What we love about Psalm 103 is that the psalmist declares the goodness of God in ways that are easy to understand. He clearly narrates what the Lord has done on our behalf. The more you read this particular psalm, the more you begin to realize that what the psalmist means by "blessing the Lord" is something like "thanking the Lord" for all of the ways that God has been good.

This psalm trains our souls, hearts, and minds to reflect on the goodness inherent in who God is, what God does, and how God cares for us. Today, our charge to you is to sit and reflect. Think of all the ways that God has been present for you. Think of the ways God has been at work behind the scenes in your life, both in ways you realize today and in ways you won't realize for years, if ever. As you think of these things, bless the Lord. Let us be clear: We want you to brag on the Lord in prayer. Tell God how dope God is. Say your prayers out loud and call out all of the ways in which God has blown your mind. This is the kind of exercise that changes your perspective and gives God what God is due! Go for it! God deserves it!

Devotional

Sharing stories about God's dopeness and God's eternal tilt toward equality waters the emotional roots of our justice imagination. Too frequently, justice talk leans on statistical analysis and theoretical arguments at the expense of our passion, our resilience, and our inner determination to work with one another in pursuit of justice.

Today, we invite you to tell God how dope God is. In your own words, name how awesome God's presence has been in your life. Don't stop at your personal life either; talk about how God has been present in your public life too. What wins for Black lives has God brought about? What victories has God led you to? Name them and celebrate them! These are the matches that will ignite your vision for a more beloved community.

Questions for the Day

- How can we go about speaking God's works and promises into our own lives? If we practice this regularly, how will it change our lives?
- "O my soul" is the psalmist's language for addressing the self. What does your soul need right now? What is your soul's deepest cry right now?

Lament

Psalm 130

Out of the depths I cry to you, O LORD.
　　Lord, hear my voice!
Let your ears be attentive
　　to the voice of my supplications!

If you, O LORD, should mark iniquities,
　　Lord, who could stand?
But there is forgiveness with you,
　　so that you may be revered.

I wait for the LORD, my soul waits,
　　and in his word I hope;
my soul waits for the Lord
　　more than those who watch for the morning,
　　more than those who watch for the morning.

O Israel, hope in the LORD!
　　For with the LORD there is steadfast love,
　　and with him is great power to redeem.
It is he who will redeem Israel
　　from all its iniquities.

Reflection

Psalm 130 is filled with a robust hope, confidence in God's love, and a reliance on God's capacity to save. It begins with an impassioned plea for divine assistance and closes with a moving statement of faith. The psalmist stirs our hearts to hope in the Lord, whose love never fails and who will redeem Israel from every kind of sin. These themes of hope and confidence nudge us to ask an urgent question: "How much do we really trust God?"

The psalmist invites us to depend on God wholeheartedly. In verse 5, we get a window into such a comprehensive faith when the psalmist proclaims, "I wait for the LORD, my soul waits, and in his word I hope." The psalmist is counting on God. He is putting all of his hope in God. Today is a great opportunity for us to do the same. If we choose, today, we can put our dreams, relationships, jobs, prayers, and our very lives, underneath God's more than capable care.

God's mercy toward us is great. God holds us together when life is difficult. Our magnificent God, full of creativity and compassion, can be trusted not only to forgive us our failures, but to fully redeem them and bring salvation into our lives. Hope in the Lord today!

Devotional

What do you need to bring before God? What dreams? What fears? What relationships and worries and unspoken needs do you need to lay at the altar? What are the things that creep into the back of your mind before you go to bed that you need to entrust to the Almighty One who is able to handle it all? Take your innermost concerns to the Lord, and while you're there, take hope in the Lord!

Pause for a moment and simply ponder. Where do you need to make adjustments in your life? Where do you need to repent? Developing a dynamic, ever-deepening justice imagination requires this kind of self-examination. It requires us to consider our role in ending white supremacy and establishing racial, gender, and economic equity. We don't just bring our personal concerns to the Lord; we bring these as well and take hope!

Questions for the Day

- Today's devotional invites us to ponder where we need to make adjustments. Where might God be calling you to make adjustments or amend your ways?

- How is your trust level with God? Think of this as a question about comprehensive trust. A justice imagination invites us to trust God not only with the immediate aspects of our life, but also with our socioeconomic, political, and collective lives. How can we build our trust in God to intervene, both directly and through human action, to repair policy legacies of racial inequality and cultural patterns of anti-blackness?

Use What You Have

Psalm 150

Praise the LORD!
Praise God in his sanctuary;
    praise him in his mighty firmament!
Praise him for his mighty deeds;
    praise him according to his surpassing greatness!

Praise him with trumpet sound;
    praise him with lute and harp!
Praise him with tambourine and dance;
    praise him with strings and pipe!
Praise him with clanging cymbals;
    praise him with loud clashing cymbals!
Let everything that breathes praise the LORD!
Praise the LORD!

Reflection

The concluding command of verse six, "Let everything that breathes praise the LORD!" closes the Psalter. It also points to the liturgical dimension of not only humanity but all creation, meaning all living beings—humans, animals in the wild, fish in the sea, birds of the air, insects—are called to praise the Lord. Everything that has breath is designed and even commanded to praise the Lord. The theological foundations for human rights, environmental concerns, and even the basic decency that undergirds civilization across cultures are all wrapped up in this psalm.

Inhale for four seconds. Exhale for four seconds. Think about how remarkable it is to receive God's graciously provided breath of life. Even the air in our lungs attests to God's abundant grace. The mere fact that our chests can expand and contract with the air that gives us life is a persistent testament to the benevolence of our Maker.

Alongside this command to praise, the psalmist also makes it clear that instruments should be used to praise the Lord. Verses 2-5 call on the tambourine, the harp, the trumpet, and many more to sound notes of praise and adoration to the Source of Life, the Source of a Healed Existence—the Author of our Salvation, the Lord. In the spirit of this psalm, may our lives, may our breath, be an instrument of praise and worship offered to a God whose loving-kindness surrounds us, supports us, covers us, and goes before us.

Devotional

Psalm 150 implies that all of life contains an element of public worship. Our justice work—the protests, the rallies, the chants, the advocacy for legislation—all of it is included in what it means for our embodied, breathing selves to praise God. In the spirit of this psalm, take five minutes to breathe in and breathe out deeply. As you inhale, breathe in God's love. As you exhale, focus your mind on how you can shower praise on the God whose justice and renewal will one day cover the earth as the waters fill the sea.

Questions for the Day

- "I can't breathe" were among the last words spoken by Eric Garner, a Black man choked to death by police on a sidewalk in Staten Island, New York. What do Garner's striking words mean in light of the psalmist's declaration, "Let everything that breathes praise the LORD"?
- Our breath is precious. Our breath is a gift. Spend a moment taking deep and intentional breaths. What comes to mind as you breathe?

You're in Charge

Psalm 8 (NLT)

O LORD, our Lord, your majestic name fills the earth!
   Your glory is higher than the heavens.
You have taught children and infants
   to tell of your strength,
   silencing your enemies
   and all who oppose you.

When I look at the night sky and see the work of your
   fingers—
   the moon and the stars you set in place—
what are mere mortals that you should think about them,
   human beings that you should care for them?
Yet you made them only a little lower than God
   and crowned them with glory and honor.
You gave them charge of everything you made,
   putting all things under their authority—
the flocks and the herds
   and all the wild animals,
the birds in the sky, the fish in the sea,
   and everything that swims the ocean currents.

O LORD, our Lord, your majestic name fills the earth!

Reflection

There's a balance that Christians have to strike between awe, wonder, and confidence. In many ways, we are awestruck by God's willingness to engage with us, or even be aware of us, when we are merely human beings. Yet we also have confidence that God wants this relationship with us and that we are special because we have been made in God's image.

Psalm 8 provides this language of reverence and awe, while also reminding us of who we are and who God has created us to be. We may not know why God thinks so highly of us, but since God does, we should think highly of ourselves as well. God wants us to remember that we've been given strength, glory, honor, and power. The same God who created the heavens and the earth has entrusted us with the responsibility to exert control over all of creation.

So chin up, child of God. Walk with your head held high! *You* have been fashioned by God. *You* have more strength than you give yourself credit for. *You* have the capacity to steward God's good creation. *You* were made just a little lower than God, and *you* are more powerful than you ever dreamed. Step into your God-given identity. The God of heaven and earth trusts *you*. It's time to trust yourself! Keep leaning on who God created you to be so that you can walk in divine strength every day of your life.

Devotional

Empowerment is your birthright as a child of God. By extension, it is also, and equally, the birthright of your family members, your friends, your neighbors, and everyone else in your community. Acknowledging and affirming this empowerment as a divine gift and a sign of the trust that God has put into each of us is essential to building an inclusive justice imagination.

As you read Psalm 8, declare your own agency. We are made a little lower than God, carrying forth an image of the Divine within our being. Walk boldly and beautifully in your God-created self.

Questions for the Day

- This psalm argues that human beings are just a little lower than God. This phrase implies that all people, by virtue of their creation by God, have inherent dignity. What does this phrase mean to you? What does it mean for all people to have inherent dignity?
- To what extent do our church and culture celebrate the divine endowment residing within each of us? What would it look like for everyone to be celebrants, eager to notice and rejoice in who God designed each of us to be?

The Lord Does That

Psalm 146

Praise the LORD!
Praise the LORD, O my soul!
I will praise the LORD as long as I live;
    I will sing praises to my God all my life long.

Do not put your trust in princes,
    in mortals, in whom there is no help.
When their breath departs, they return to the earth;
    on that very day their plans perish.

Happy are those whose help is the God of Jacob,
    whose hope is in the LORD their God,
who made heaven and earth,
    the sea, and all that is in them;
who keeps faith forever;
    who executes justice for the oppressed;
    who gives food to the hungry.

The LORD sets the prisoners free;
    the LORD opens the eyes of the blind.
The LORD lifts up those who are bowed down;
    the LORD loves the righteous.
The LORD watches over the strangers;

he upholds the orphan and the widow,
    but the way of the wicked he brings to ruin.

The LORD will reign forever,
    your God, O Zion, for all generations.
Praise the LORD!

Reflection

Psalm 146 is, in colloquial terms, a whole blessing. It covers everything from divine help to the power of praise to, crucially, God's role in providing justice. Verses 7-8 underscore the latter theme, declaring that the Lord "executes justice for the oppressed" and "gives food to the hungry." The psalmist then continues by proclaiming that, "The LORD sets the prisoners free; the LORD opens the eyes of the blind. The LORD lifts up those who are bowed down."

Reading these verses invites a sense of awe, but also confusion. How does an unseen God provide justice, food, freedom, sight, and uplift to those who need it? While the psalmist affirms that God does this work, he declines to provide an explanation for how it takes place. Søren Kierkegaard offers a perspective that may shed some light on the passage when he posits that "Life must be understood backwards; but . . . it must be lived forwards." While this does not clarify our conundrum, it makes sense of our inability to know the answer.

When thinking about hunger, injustice, and oppression in the abstract, it is not always clear that God is moving to intervene for the common good. However, when looking back in retrospect, the testimonies that attribute victory and survival over collective evil and social harm to a divine source are plentiful. The autobiographies of civil rights leaders, former slaves, apartheid activists, and other artisans of the beloved community bear a similar witness. The Lord of heaven and earth makes a way. The Lord of heaven and earth brings forth justice within corrupt political orders, inspires the growth and impact of social movements, and protects the lives and resources of vulnerable communities.

Let us join with the psalmist and sing praise to God until our dying breath, for the Lord who "executes justice for the oppressed" is the first and the final cause—although not the sole cause, for people must still play their part—of the liberation and laughter that we can enjoy in this life, as well as in the life to come.

Devotional

Today's devotion is a "before and after" exercise designed to help foster a justice imagination. Consider an experience from the past where God's justice was not evident at the time. Consider what it would have sounded like in the moment to declare that God was at work. What emotions would it have prompted? Would it have been hard to believe? Now, think of the same experience, knowing what you know now. Does your present understanding provide a different angle to think about what happened? Are there ways of understanding how the Lord was at work at the time that you can see now, but which were hidden as things happened at the time?

Write down two or three ways that God could have been operating behind the scenes. Cultivating a justice imagination means trusting that God's spirit is ushering us, often unaware, toward the common good in times and places where we least expect it. In the tradition of this psalm, and in the hope of advancing God's liberation among those counted least in our society, continue to develop your justice imagination today.

Questions for the Day

- Cultivating a justice imagination means we visualize the Spirit ushering us toward a common good. As you reflect on this idea, visualize a time where God executed justice for the oppressed, gave food to the hungry, or set the prisoners free. What did it look like to see God put justice into action?
- What does it mean to be ushered toward a common good? How do we make space to celebrate God's work of justice in our midst?

Teach Us to Count Our Days

Psalm 90

Lord, you have been our dwelling place
    in all generations.
Before the mountains were brought forth,
    or ever you had formed the earth and the world,
    from everlasting to everlasting you are God.

You turn us back to dust,
    and say, "Turn back, you mortals."
For a thousand years in your sight
    are like yesterday when it is past,
    or like a watch in the night.

You sweep them away; they are like a dream,
    like grass that is renewed in the morning;
in the morning it flourishes and is renewed;
    in the evening it fades and withers.

For we are consumed by your anger;
    by your wrath we are overwhelmed.
You have set our iniquities before you,
    our secret sins in the light of your countenance.

For all our days pass away under your wrath;
    our years come to an end like a sigh.
The days of our life are seventy years,
    or perhaps eighty, if we are strong;
even then their span is only toil and trouble;
    they are soon gone, and we fly away.

Who considers the power of your anger?
    Your wrath is as great as the fear that is due you.
So teach us to count our days
    that we may gain a wise heart.

Turn, O LORD! How long?
    Have compassion on your servants!
Satisfy us in the morning with your steadfast love,
    so that we may rejoice and be glad all our days.
Make us glad as many days as you have afflicted us,
    and as many years as we have seen evil.
Let your work be manifest to your servants,
    and your glorious power to their children.
Let the favor of the LORD our God be upon us,
    and prosper for us the work of our hands—
    O prosper the work of our hands!

Reflection

In the words of Psalm 90, the Lord has been our dwelling place throughout all generations. From the days of the brush harbor, where many of our enslaved ancestors called on the name of Christ in the American South, to the Great Awakening, to the days of the Civil War and Reconstruction, to the transformative Black church piety that informed much of the

Civil Rights movement, God has indeed been our home, a refuge, a dwelling place for Christians of African descent. The simple, profound truth of this confession is that the Ancient of Days is faithful, dependable, and ever-present.

Within the sociocultural marks of history, the psalmist makes a theological claim about God's transcendence beyond time in verse 2 proclaiming that "from everlasting to everlasting you are God." It is comforting to confess that the author of time envelops the journey of our lives with eternal care. Our traumas and triumphs, our resentments, which are not easily shaken, and the great causes to which we are called all exist within the grace of God.

With the rising of the sun each day, we ask God to, "Satisfy us in the morning with your steadfast love" (v. 14). As we carry out the duties of our waking lives, we pray to the God who mothers us with the words of wisdom traditionally ascribed to Moses when we ask God to "teach us to count our days, that we may gain a wise heart" (v. 12). And once the moonlight's sweeping glow replaces the sunshine, we lift up our voices with the psalmist and pray, "Let the favor of the LORD our God be upon us, and prosper for us the work of our hands—O prosper the work of our hands!" (v. 17).

Devotional

When we listen to the God who is our dwelling place and to those in the communities where we dwell, we forge a justice imagination rooted in relationship with God *and* with our neighbors. At the nexus of that interconnected relationship, the place where our deeds bless other folks, God smiles upon our labor.

Take fifteen minutes in discerning prayer, asking the Holy Spirit to reveal how your work blesses others. Write down whatever revelations emerge. Write out the emotions or ideas you experience during this time of prayer. Conclude your prayer time by asking God to lead you further into the meeting ground of fair treatment and faithful action, the intersection where, as the psalmist says, God can prosper the work of your hands.

Questions for the Day

- Have you seen God prosper the work of your hands for the collective benefit of the community? What happened?
- If you have seen this, what did you do to celebrate that? How can you celebrate this with others?
- If you haven't seen this happen, what does it look like to rejoice in expectation that God will bless the work of your hands in the future?

Pray for Our Leaders

Psalm 72

Give the king your justice, O God,
    and your righteousness to a king's son.
May he judge your people with righteousness,
    and your poor with justice.
May the mountains yield prosperity for the people,
    and the hills, in righteousness.
May he defend the cause of the poor of the people,
    give deliverance to the needy,
    and crush the oppressor.

May he live while the sun endures,
    and as long as the moon, throughout all generations.
May he be like rain that falls on the mown grass,
    like showers that water the earth.
In his days may righteousness flourish
    and peace abound, until the moon is no more.

May he have dominion from sea to sea,
    and from the River to the ends of the earth.
May his foes bow down before him,
    and his enemies lick the dust.
May the kings of Tarshish and of the isles
    render him tribute,

may the kings of Sheba and Seba
    bring gifts.
May all kings fall down before him,
    all nations give him service.

For he delivers the needy when they call,
    the poor and those who have no helper.
He has pity on the weak and the needy,
    and saves the lives of the needy.
From oppression and violence he redeems their life;
    and precious is their blood in his sight.

Long may he live!
    May gold of Sheba be given to him.
May prayer be made for him continually,
    and blessings invoked for him all day long.
May there be abundance of grain in the land;
    may it wave on the tops of the mountains;
    may its fruit be like Lebanon;
and may people blossom in the cities
    like the grass of the field.
May his name endure forever,
    his fame continue as long as the sun.
May all nations be blessed in him;
    may they pronounce him happy.

Blessed be the LORD, the God of Israel,
    who alone does wondrous things.
Blessed be his glorious name forever;
    may his glory fill the whole earth.
Amen and Amen.

The prayers of David son of Jesse are ended.

Reflection

Psalm 72 is the most extensive meditation on the moral imperatives of political authority in the entire Psalter. Despite being written in the context of the empires and monarchies of the ancient Near East, its insights remain relevant in an age of so-called established and emerging democracies. Consider the opening line, "Give the king your justice, O God." These opening words speak to a desire and determination to truly see justice done, rather than paying lip service and virtue signaling about the importance of justice. Relating it back to our context, it is important that our systems of government implement public policy in a way that demonstrates that Black lives matter rather than performing solely symbolic gestures that make no difference in community health and the lived experiences of Black people.

Deeper still, this psalm suggests that political authority is similar to divine authority. Matters of life and death reside in the realms of politics, the law, and government. We witness this on one hand in the conduct of the military, police, prisons, and detention centers, and on the other, in the degree of access provided to public health resources, educational opportunity, clean environments, and decent housing. God remains the fundamental arbiter of existence and destiny for human beings, but the primary stewards of life and death in a society are an overlapping network of social movement actors, government staff, civil society organizations, and everyday citizens. In this sense, verse 1 is a plea and prayer for political authority—in the psalmist's case, a king—to approximate God's authority by governing with a steadfast commitment to justice, not merely order.

The psalmist envisions the ideal king as someone who is responsible for treating the poor fairly (v. 2), rescuing the children of the needy (v. 4), and presiding over conditions where peace is abundant (v. 7). These tasks are more than a checklist or a job description for the king. Instead, they are the expectations of what an ethical political authority looks like.

Notably, Psalm 72 combines the genres of prayer, lament, and social criticism. Following in this tradition, let us join the writer in praying for political authority whose leadership is "refreshing like spring rain on freshly cut grass, like showers that water the earth" (v. 6).

Devotional

Though written in a different social context, this psalm resonates in our modern political landscape. In every election season, across every public administration, the prayer of the psalmist is our petition. As we lift up this prayer, our justice imagination overcomes the false division of sacred and secular, integrating all of our reality into our ethical horizon and devotional life.

In that spirit, let us pray together saying, "Gracious Lord, guide our countries and communities into racial equity and genuine peace using leaders whose impact is 'refreshing like spring rain on freshly cut grass, like showers that water the earth.'" (v. 6)

Questions for the Day

- The psalm contends that political authority can, at least in part, mediate divine justice. What examples of contemporary political authority, if any, suggest that the Lord can use people and human governments to advance justice? How can these examples be celebrated?

- While examples to the contrary abound, preserving the positive experiences helps foster a justice imagination by celebrating moments where God works through imperfect political bodies. What does it look like to celebrate these moments while still acknowledging the flaws of our political systems?

Steadfast

Psalm 118

O give thanks to the LORD, for he is good;
   his steadfast love endures forever!

Let Israel say,
   "His steadfast love endures forever."
Let the house of Aaron say,
   "His steadfast love endures forever."
Let those who fear the LORD say,
   "His steadfast love endures forever."

Out of my distress I called on the LORD;
   the LORD answered me and set me in a broad place.
With the LORD on my side I do not fear.
   What can mortals do to me?
The LORD is on my side to help me;
   I shall look in triumph on those who hate me.
It is better to take refuge in the LORD
   than to put confidence in mortals.
It is better to take refuge in the LORD
   than to put confidence in princes.

All nations surrounded me;
   in the name of the LORD I cut them off!

They surrounded me, surrounded me on every side;
    in the name of the LORD I cut them off!
They surrounded me like bees;
    they blazed like a fire of thorns;
    in the name of the LORD I cut them off!
I was pushed hard, so that I was falling,
    but the LORD helped me.
The LORD is my strength and my might;
    he has become my salvation.

There are glad songs of victory in the tents of the righteous:
"The right hand of the LORD does valiantly;
    the right hand of the LORD is exalted;
    the right hand of the LORD does valiantly."
I shall not die, but I shall live,
    and recount the deeds of the LORD.
The LORD has punished me severely,
    but he did not give me over to death.

Open to me the gates of righteousness,
    that I may enter through them
    and give thanks to the LORD.

This is the gate of the LORD;
    the righteous shall enter through it.

I thank you that you have answered me
    and have become my salvation.
The stone that the builders rejected
    has become the chief cornerstone.
This is the LORD's doing;
    it is marvelous in our eyes.

This is the day that the LORD has made;
    let us rejoice and be glad in it.
Save us, we beseech you, O LORD!
    O LORD, we beseech you, give us success!

Blessed is the one who comes in the name of the LORD.
    We bless you from the house of the LORD.
The LORD is God,
    and he has given us light.
Bind the festal procession with branches,
    up to the horns of the altar.

You are my God, and I will give thanks to you;
    you are my God, I will extol you.

O give thanks to the LORD, for he is good,
    for his steadfast love endures forever.

Reflection

The psalmist reminds us that God's steadfast love endures forever. What a needed testimony! In hard times, our experiences stir up doubts about whether God truly cares for us, but here we are reminded about the good news that the divine pledge of *hesed*, of loving-kindness for humanity and all creation, is ever-present.

Psalm 118 also supplies us with a staple call to worship in many Black church services, "This is the day that the LORD has made, let us rejoice and be glad in it" (v. 24). Here is the key to resilient, jubilant spirituality. Each day emerges from God's handiwork; each day contains reasons and incentives for joy, for gratitude, and for well-considered celebration.

As you navigate today's obligations, expectations, and aspirations, take some time to rejoice. Rejoice in the morning, rejoice at noon, and rejoice throughout the evening. Take time to remind yourself that today, no matter its jagged edges and frustrations, is indeed a day that the Lord has made.

God authors time and existence anew each day and supplies us with breath to live and strength to love. This means we have sufficient reason each day to forge a unique pathway to gladness in the realities of our lives. To modify a sentiment of James Baldwin, one of our great Black bards, our crown of joy has already been bought and paid for. Let us adjust our crowns for the day and stride toward God's freedom.

Devotional

Make an appointment today for joy. Joy and gladness, no less than moral indignation, are part of stewarding a healthy justice imagination. Just like we schedule everything from healthcare visits to protests, joy deserves its own calendar invite. Grab twenty minutes today—or whatever you can manage—to sit silently, savoring what Rabbi Abraham Heschel calls the "radical amazement" of being alive.

Questions for the Day

- The psalmist commands us to rejoice in the Lord and be glad in the day of the Lord. What would it look like to embody an inclusive gladness, big enough to incorporate days that are entirely joyful as well as days shot through with pain, suffering, and institutional sin?

- How might our understanding of gladness evolve if we tried to capture the polarities of human experience within its confines? What does it mean to be glad during hard times?

When God Feels Far Away

Psalm 22

My God, my God, why have you forsaken me?
Why are you so far from helping me, from the words of my
    groaning?
O my God, I cry by day, but you do not answer;
    and by night, but find no rest.

Yet you are holy,
    enthroned on the praises of Israel.
In you our ancestors trusted;
    they trusted, and you delivered them.
To you they cried, and were saved;
    in you they trusted, and were not put to shame.

But I am a worm, and not human;
    scorned by others, and despised by the people.
All who see me mock at me;
    they make mouths at me, they shake their heads;
"Commit your cause to the LORD; let him deliver—
    let him rescue the one in whom he delights!"

Yet it was you who took me from the womb;
    you kept me safe on my mother's breast.
On you I was cast from my birth,

and since my mother bore me you have been my God.
Do not be far from me,
    for trouble is near
    and there is no one to help.

Many bulls encircle me,
    strong bulls of Bashan surround me;
they open wide their mouths at me,
    like a ravening and roaring lion.

I am poured out like water,
    and all my bones are out of joint;
my heart is like wax;
    it is melted within my breast;
my mouth is dried up like a potsherd,
    and my tongue sticks to my jaws;
    you lay me in the dust of death.

For dogs are all around me;
    a company of evildoers encircles me.
My hands and feet have shriveled;
I can count all my bones.
They stare and gloat over me;
they divide my clothes among themselves,
    and for my clothing they cast lots.

But you, O LORD, do not be far away!
    O my help, come quickly to my aid!
Deliver my soul from the sword,
    my life from the power of the dog!
    Save me from the mouth of the lion!

From the horns of the wild oxen you have rescued me.
I will tell of your name to my brothers and sisters;
 in the midst of the congregation I will praise you:
You who fear the LORD, praise him!
 All you offspring of Jacob, glorify him;
 stand in awe of him, all you offspring of Israel!
For he did not despise or abhor
 the affliction of the afflicted;
he did not hide his face from me,
 but heard when I cried to him.

From you comes my praise in the great congregation;
 my vows I will pay before those who fear him.
The poor shall eat and be satisfied;
 those who seek him shall praise the LORD.
 May your hearts live forever!

All the ends of the earth shall remember
 and turn to the LORD;
and all the families of the nations
 shall worship before him.
For dominion belongs to the LORD,
 and he rules over the nations.

To him, indeed, shall all who sleep in the earth bow down;
 before him shall bow all who go down to the dust,
 and I shall live for him.
Posterity will serve him;
 future generations will be told about the Lord,
and proclaim his deliverance to a people yet unborn,
 saying that he has done it.

Reflection

Psalm 22 is, in part, a meditation on faith and childhood. Verses 9-10 declare, "Yet it was you who took me from the womb; you kept me safe on my mother's breast. On you I was cast from my birth, and since my mother bore me you have been my God."

How often do we mark our divine-human connection to the time of our birth, to a time before attending church, before memorizing scripture, before a confession of faith? All those moments are important, but the psalmist seizes on an elemental aspect of faith. Our primordial encounters with God *precede* our later articulation of what God means to us. Before we could use language, before we even knew what language was, a Loving Presence brought us into existence from our mother's womb. Surrounded by petitions for divine aid, vows of praise, and poignantly expressed despair, the psalmist smuggles in this dash of retrospective awe when he says, "Since my mother bore me you have been my God." The same is true for us. We can also retrieve these memories of God in our first moments, before our first moments, and use them as a defense against environmental and social harms, as a source of devotion that undergirds our connection to our Creator and to our self.

Indeed, from a certain perspective, our childhoods illustrate God's faithfulness. We continue to move from one stage of development to another, and the mere fact of our survival, despite the violence, internalized insults, and whatever else a cruel world can throw against us, attests to God's sustaining power. By grace, that blend of divine agency and historical circumstance, we have, in the words of a much favored song in the Black church, come this far by faith, leaning on the Lord.

From the day of your birth to this present day, from your mother's womb until this very hour, we have been parented by a grace-filled God. With that recognition, let us praise our Creator and Caregiver, taking our cues from the psalmist who declares, "I will tell of your name to my brothers and sisters; in the midst of the congregation I will praise you" (v. 22).

Devotional

Our survival from childhood to this moment—despite the triple scourge of racism, sexism, and capitalism—attests to God's sustaining power. Appreciating the fact of our survival and crediting God with that survival is a critical theological dimension of building our justice imagination. The claim rests on a simple fact: Our survival is a precondition for pursuing justice of any sort.

Take inventory of your own life. What have you survived? What seasons have you endured in the past? Surveying those moments, name at least one thing that they suggest about the preserving power of God.

Questions for the Day

- The psalmist narrates an experience of divine rescue followed by praise. What does it look like to celebrate God's presence and supernatural assistance? What moments of rescue do we have to praise God for?
- Take a moment to name, narrate, and celebrate instances where God's mighty acts have transformed your vulnerabilities into victories. Over time, celebrate and commemorate wins as a way to foster your justice imagination.

Down Through the Years

Psalm 71

In you, O Lord, I take refuge;
    let me never be put to shame.
In your righteousness deliver me and rescue me;
    incline your ear to me and save me.
Be to me a rock of refuge,
    a strong fortress, to save me,
    for you are my rock and my fortress.

Rescue me, O my God, from the hand of the wicked,
    from the grasp of the unjust and cruel.
For you, O Lord, are my hope,
    my trust, O Lord, from my youth.
Upon you I have leaned from my birth;
    it was you who took me from my mother's womb.
My praise is continually of you.

I have been like a portent to many,
    but you are my strong refuge.
My mouth is filled with your praise,
    and with your glory all day long.
Do not cast me off in the time of old age;
    do not forsake me when my strength is spent.

For my enemies speak concerning me,
 and those who watch for my life consult together.
They say, "Pursue and seize that person
 whom God has forsaken,
  for there is no one to deliver."

O God, do not be far from me;
 O my God, make haste to help me!
Let my accusers be put to shame and consumed;
 let those who seek to hurt me
  be covered with scorn and disgrace.
But I will hope continually,
 and will praise you yet more and more.
My mouth will tell of your righteous acts,
 of your deeds of salvation all day long,
  though their number is past my knowledge.
I will come praising the mighty deeds of the Lord God,
 I will praise your righteousness, yours alone.

O God, from my youth you have taught me,
 and I still proclaim your wondrous deeds.
So even to old age and gray hairs,
 O God, do not forsake me,
until I proclaim your might
 to all the generations to come.
Your power [19] and your righteousness, O God,
 reach the high heavens.

You who have done great things,
 O God, who is like you?
You who have made me see many troubles and calamities
 will revive me again;

from the depths of the earth
    you will bring me up again.
You will increase my honor,
    and comfort me once again.

I will also praise you with the harp
    for your faithfulness, O my God;
I will sing praises to you with the lyre,
    O Holy One of Israel.
My lips will shout for joy
    when I sing praises to you;
    my soul also, which you have rescued.
All day long my tongue will talk of your righteous help,
for those who tried to do me harm
    have been put to shame, and disgraced.

Reflection

Psalm 71 is a psalm about the stages of life. It captures the spectrum of human experience from infancy to older adulthood. Reflecting on the earliest stages of life in verses 5-6, the psalmist muses, "For you, O LORD, are my hope, my trust, O LORD, from my youth. Upon you I have leaned from my birth; it was you who took me from my mother's womb. My praise is continually of you." This almost prenatal trust in the Lord, leading to a deep-seated praise of God, is on full display in these verses. Indeed, if we look hard enough, all of us can affirm on some level that God has cared for us since we were in the womb.

Following this, the psalmist pivots to the perspective of a community elder in verse 18. The psalmist maintains, "So even to old age and gray hairs, O God, do not forsake me, until I proclaim your might to all the generations to come." There's a connection between the faith expressed during the early and later stages of life, between the recognition that "It was you who took me from my mother's womb," and the impassioned plea, "So even to old age and gray hairs, O God, do not forsake me." Over the course of our lives, there's a bridge we must travel to enjoy our deepest, most fulfilling journey of faith in God. This bridge is a pathway of introspection, slow thinking, and prayer before God's presence.

After a lifetime of communion with God, a life spent petitioning the Lord for deliverance from "the hand of the wicked, from the grasp of the unjust and cruel" (v. 4), the psalmist leaves a legacy of faith. His message to us is to trust God throughout the successive phases of life's journey and the places it takes us. God's power and miracles are present within every predicament of life. However deep the oppression may be, God is present to heal, present to empower, and present to make impossible ventures doable by the power of faith.

Devotional

Take fifteen minutes to both name social evils and reflect on the nature of God, using the following structure: "X social evil is real, but so is God's Y." For instance, "White supremacy is real, but so is God's love for justice." Or, "Stained-glass sexism is real, but so is God's Spirit poured out on all flesh." Consider the last five years of your life. What social evils have felt especially real during this time? Over the same period of time, name an aspect of God's character that has also felt real to you. Use your reflections to engage in the exercise of voicing social evils and reflecting on God's character. The powers and principalities are real, but so is the Lord of hosts!

Questions for the Day

- We often believe that God's deeds of deliverance and salvation are limited, unusual, or interruptions from the status quo. The psalmist argues the opposite. Psalm 71 asserts that God's deeds of salvation are too many to number. Where have you seen God's work of deliverance and salvation recently? Don't overlook even the smallest moments.
- Inspired by God's work of salvation, consider what it would look like for God to work through the church to heal, bless, build, and advocate toward a just, equitable future. What can you do to bring this future to reality? What can the church do? How can we celebrate joining in God's work?

They're Ganging up on Me

Psalm 3 (NLT)

O LORD, I have so many enemies;
   so many are against me.
So many are saying,
   "God will never rescue him!"   *Interlude*

But you, O LORD, are a shield around me;
   you are my glory, the one who holds my head high.
I cried out to the LORD,
   and he answered me from his holy mountain.   *Interlude*

I lay down and slept,
   yet I woke up in safety,
   for the LORD was watching over me.
I am not afraid of ten thousand enemies
   who surround me on every side.

Arise, O LORD!
   Rescue me, my God!
Slap all my enemies in the face!
   Shatter the teeth of the wicked!
Victory comes from you, O LORD.
   May you bless your people.   *Interlude*

Reflection

God is a shield around the faithful (v. 3). For believers, God provides a psychological buffer, a hedge of protection, holding our minds and spirits in safety and security. There is another sense in which God shields us, however. God uses our communities and, occasionally, events within history—such as social movements, revivals, worship services, miracles, and sacred writings—to send protection. Thank God for defending our lives!

Enjoying divine protection, however, does not exclude us from pain, harm, or making mistakes. Divine protection, instead, means that when we cry out to the Lord, God supplies an answer from God's holy mountain (v. 4). We don't avoid the pain, but sometimes we learn a lesson within it. Rather than getting around a troubling circumstance, protection sometimes means *going through it* and developing character, self-determination, and inventiveness—that precious skill of making much with little and seeing possibilities where others see dead ends.

God is our protection through dangers seen and unseen, oppressions named and unnamed. Who else could inspire, using the terms of Black church historian and theologian Gayraud Wilmore, *survival, uplift,* and, at times, even *liberation,* among Black diasporic peoples? The Spirit who catalyzed freedom from colonial regimes, Jim Crow, and chattel slavery is the Spirit who animates abolitionist movements against police and prisons. This Spirit is also our ever-present help, the one who is our glory, who holds our head high.

Our glorious God displays care in grand events, to be sure, but also in our most intimate moments. The psalmist

highlights the divine attribute of tenderness in verse five saying, "I lay down and slept, yet I woke up on safety, for the
LORD was watching over me." What a fitting anthem for our
discipleship. We awake each day because the God of our hope
sustains us. When our labors are done, God protects us as
we lie down for slumber. We are surrounded, indwelt, and
beloved by a great God, nearer to us than our own breath,
close enough to feel, to trust.

Devotional

Today's devotion is designed to weave an abiding trust in
divine protection more deeply into our justice imagination.

Pull up a blank page and make a list of five things that
are causing a sense of vulnerability in your community. After
writing them out, slowly make a circle around each response
you listed.

Next, create a larger circle that encompasses all of the
responses you've written. Take a deep breath. Look at each
circle, first the smaller ones, then the larger one. Imagine that
these circles represent God's loving protection. What does it
mean for God to protect us from these concerns? What does
it look like to trust God with these worries? Finally, retrace
each of your circles again, the larger first, and then the smaller
ones. As you do, say a prayer trusting that God's peace, as the
apostle Paul maintains, will guard your heart and mind in
Christ Jesus.

Questions for the Day

- Who do you envision is on your side in life? How do you define who your enemies are?

- Have your family members ever been enemies? This psalm was written by David during a time when he was running for his life because his son wanted his throne. Sometimes the hearts of our families can become corrupted, and those we love can turn on us. David models that even in these times, we can still pray. How do you typically respond to attacks from within your family?

- What does it look like to pray for God's protection in all things? What does it look like to arm yourself with the promises of God?

- You're going to make it out. God has you. What does escape look like? What does a win look like for you?

When Your Soul Is Discouraged

Psalm 42 (NLT)

As the deer longs for streams of water,
    so I long for you, O God.
I thirst for God, the living God.
    When can I go and stand before him?
Day and night I have only tears for food,
    while my enemies continually taunt me, saying,
    "Where is this God of yours?"

My heart is breaking
    as I remember how it used to be:
I walked among the crowds of worshipers,
    leading a great procession to the house of God,
singing for joy and giving thanks
    amid the sound of a great celebration!

Why am I discouraged?
    Why is my heart so sad?
I will put my hope in God!
    I will praise him again—
    my Savior and [6] my God!

Now I am deeply discouraged,
    but I will remember you—

80

even from distant Mount Hermon, the source of the Jordan,
    from the land of Mount Mizar.
I hear the tumult of the raging seas
    as your waves and surging tides sweep over me.
But each day the LORD pours his unfailing love upon me,
    and through each night I sing his songs,
    praying to God who gives me life.

"O God my rock," I cry,
    "Why have you forgotten me?
Why must I wander around in grief,
    oppressed by my enemies?"
Their taunts break my bones.
    They scoff, "Where is this God of yours?"

Why am I discouraged?
    Why is my heart so sad?
I will put my hope in God!
    I will praise him again—
    my Savior and my God!

Reflection

Our need for the Holy One is like a deer's thirst for water—irresistible. The psalmist underscores this point in verse 2 saying, "I thirst for God, the living God. Where can I go and stand before him?" There's a core image of survival and human dependence on God that bursts from this psalm. As plants need sunlight, as fire needs oxygen, so humans need God. The hunt for transcendence, even when God isn't directly invoked, finds expression in the arts, in nature, and even in politics. It cannot be avoided, only repressed, and then only for a moment. As a deer longs for the stream, so our souls long for God.

An aesthetic reading of this psalm strengthens our attachment to God by focusing on the beauty, joy, and emotional pull of our communion with our Creator. The psalmist surveys history and memory to unearth the pleasures of worship. In verse 4, the psalmist reflects, "I remember how it used to be: I walked among the crowds of worshipers, leading a great procession to the house of God, singing for joy and giving thanks amid the sound of a great celebration!" Joyful singing, giving thanks, and spirited celebration are not actions done out of obligation. Instead, this behavior reflects a surge of enjoyment and a group of people who are savoring the presence of God.

Articulating the love of God in our hearts helps us to trust, listen, and follow the Lord more deeply. This is a principal goal of the spiritual life for Christians. Let your heart, informed by this psalm, tilt your being toward God. Let God's power emerge within you. In the fitting words of the psalmist, declare that, "Each day the LORD pours his unfailing love upon me, and through each night I sing his songs, praying to God who gives me life" (v. 8).

Devotional

Taking a cue from the psalmist, consider your emotional history with God. What images best describe your religious experiences? What feelings come to mind? Joy and awe, hurt and pain, something else? As individuals living within what Audre Lorde once called an "anti-erotic society," articulating our emotional relationship with God is a theologically rebellious practice that reclaims the heart and affections of our justice imagination.

Set aside ten minutes to create your own word cloud comprised of words and phrases that capture your emotional connections to God. Hold onto your word cloud, and consult it periodically for inspiration and introspection.

Questions for the Day

- What are you truly thirsty for? Are you comfortable being honest with yourself about what your soul craves? Have you ever been made to feel guilty for being thirsty? What did that do to your confidence? Did it make you insecure about owning what you want?
- Does your soul long for something more than it longs for God? How can you align your desires so that your desire for God is always stronger than your desire for other things?
- What is your deepest need when you are downcast? Is it love? Is it affirmation? Is it acceptance? What tends to help you find your way after something has crushed your spirit?
- What does it look like to envision yourself being honest, vulnerable, transparent, and loved?

In Need of Mercy

Psalm 51

Have mercy on me, O God,
    according to your steadfast love;
according to your abundant mercy
    blot out my transgressions.
Wash me thoroughly from my iniquity,
    and cleanse me from my sin.

For I know my transgressions,
    and my sin is ever before me.
Against you, you alone, have I sinned,
    and done what is evil in your sight,
so that you are justified in your sentence
    and blameless when you pass judgment.
Indeed, I was born guilty,
    a sinner when my mother conceived me.

You desire truth in the inward being;
    therefore teach me wisdom in my secret heart.
Purge me with hyssop, and I shall be clean;
    wash me, and I shall be whiter than snow.
Let me hear joy and gladness;
    let the bones that you have crushed rejoice.

Hide your face from my sins,
    and blot out all my iniquities.

Create in me a clean heart, O God,
    and put a new and right spirit within me.
Do not cast me away from your presence,
    and do not take your holy spirit from me.
Restore to me the joy of your salvation,
    and sustain in me a willing spirit.

Then I will teach transgressors your ways,
    and sinners will return to you.
Deliver me from bloodshed, O God,
    O God of my salvation,
    and my tongue will sing aloud of your deliverance.

O Lord, open my lips,
    and my mouth will declare your praise.
For you have no delight in sacrifice;
    if I were to give a burnt offering, you would not be
    pleased.
The sacrifice acceptable to God is a broken spirit;
    a broken and contrite heart, O God, you will not
    despise.

Do good to Zion in your good pleasure;
    rebuild the walls of Jerusalem,
then you will delight in right sacrifices,
    in burnt offerings and whole burnt offerings;
    then bulls will be offered on your altar.

Reflection

Contrition and reform are crucial aspects of the spiritual life. Faith eventually requires all of us to confess error, to name our faults before God, and to seek counsel to correct our ways. Psalm 51 is one of the penitential psalms and describes the architecture of repentance in clear, accessible ways. The psalmist opens verse 1 with the plea, "Have mercy on me, O God, according to your steadfast love; according to your abundant mercy blot out my transgressions."

Notice the appeal to God's character. The Lord is described as possessing "steadfast love" and "abundant mercy." In the throes of transgressions and spiritual neglect, God holds us accountable with a merciful spirit. Our Divine Mother requires the observance of moral law, while also catching us with pardon, forgiveness, and restoration when we stumble.

The ultimate aim of repentance is not abstract rightness. The aim, instead, is to experience newness of heart and a reset of whatever relationships may have been damaged by our actions against people, against nature, and ultimately against God. The psalmist expresses this desire most strongly in verse 10 crying, "Create in me a clean heart, O God, and put a new and right spirit within me." May the psalmist's prayer be our own, so that after all of our transgressions, moral failures, and ethical shortcomings, we might experience the Lord's most choice gifts to a soul aggrieved by sin, "the joy of our salvation" (v. 12).

Devotional

Confessing our sins is a crucial practice for a faithful, justice-oriented life. What sins—personal and collective—do you need to confess?

Ask the Spirit to search you, elevating your part in wrongdoing to your attention. As areas emerge within your heart and mind, admit your error. It's also just as important that you accept God's forgiveness and make a plan to set it right by repairing relationships and redressing any harm that was done.

Questions for the Day

- There are times when we know what we've done was wrong. The critical question is what happens when we realize it. When you've done something wrong, how do you assess and correct course? How do you avoid letting yourself off the hook?
- What does it look like to live in a world where you don't have to be perfect, but you do have to own your mistakes?
- When you apologize, how do you fully take stock of the wrong you've caused and truly commit not to harm again? How do you receive apologies from others?

I Will Worship You

Psalm 95 (NLT)

Come, let us sing to the LORD!
  Let us shout joyfully to the Rock of our salvation.
Let us come to him with thanksgiving.
  Let us sing psalms of praise to him.
For the LORD is a great God,
  a great King above all gods.
He holds in his hands the depths of the earth
  and the mightiest mountains.
The sea belongs to him, for he made it.
  His hands formed the dry land, too.

Come, let us worship and bow down.
  Let us kneel before the LORD our maker,
  for he is our God.
We are the people he watches over,
  the flock under his care.

If only you would listen to his voice today!
The LORD says, "Don't harden your hearts as Israel did at
  Meribah,
  as they did at Massah in the wilderness.

For there your ancestors tested and tried my patience,
    even though they saw everything I did.
For forty years I was angry with them, and I said,
'They are a people whose hearts turn away from me.
    They refuse to do what I tell them.'
So in my anger I took an oath:
    'They will never enter my place of rest.' "

Reflection

This psalm retains a special place in the life of Black churches, perhaps all churches throughout the Christian communion. In such settings, it is not uncommon to hear the summons, "Come, let us worship and bow down. Let us kneel before the Lord our Maker, for he is our God. We are the people he watches over, the flock under his care" (v. 6-7). The brevity of these words merits a close examination to unearth their depth. The Lord is not only our Maker and Creator, but also our God who intimately protects, preserves, and loves us as "the people he watches over, the flock under his care."

Whether the agricultural imagery grips us or not, whether the gendered language for the Divine arrests our attention or not, the core message is this: God brings us into the world and protects us while we inhabit it. We serve a higher power who is willing to roll up their sleeves to find us when we're lost, defend us when we're endangered, and feed us when we're hungry. What a mighty God we serve! For the faithful, neither our good experiences, nor our close brushes with disaster are incidental stories. They are the result of a powerful, personal being—a very present help, as the psalmist puts it in Psalm 46—tending to our needs in times of both trouble and triumph.

This psalm concludes with a warning to heed God's voice. The psalmist implores us not to harden our hearts through non-responsiveness and spiritual neglect when we hear the voice of the Holy (v. 8). It's an appropriate end to a worship-oriented psalm. Every biblical summons to worship contains an ethical edge. For every passage that marvels at God's character, there is a corresponding call to honor God through our lives. Within this psalm, the opening emphasis on giving thanks and kneeling before our Maker transitions into the action-oriented challenge to heed God's voice, dare to live by it, and, ultimately, discover a divine rest. Today, let our hearts embrace this challenge and worship God while also walking in the way that God calls us.

Devotional

Kneeling before our Maker sometimes requires setting what management scholar Peter Drucker calls "posteriorities." These are the tasks that we have to decide not to do. These are the things that we have to determine are better handled by someone else. In a social sense, establishing posteriorities builds our justice imagination by instilling a deeper appreciation for the division of labor in a community. Simply put, we aren't called to be solo crusaders in the quest to undo anti-blackness and establish racial justice. Everyone, and all groups, have a role to play in this sacred, collective undertaking.

Take at least ten minutes to kneel before God today. Silently meditate on the thought that you can establish, through a combination of effort and God's deep and abundant grace, your own priorities and posteriorities, and work for a fair division of labor in your community.

Questions for the Day

- What does it look like to have a tender heart? How does this shape a justice imagination?
- What has caused you to put up emotional walls in the past? Are there conditions that you can envision that would help you tear down those walls?
- What does vulnerable love look like to you? How we can we love God vulnerably?

Delight in the Lord

Psalm 19

The heavens are telling the glory of God;
    and the firmament proclaims his handiwork.
Day to day pours forth speech,
    and night to night declares knowledge.
There is no speech, nor are there words;
    their voice is not heard;
yet their voice goes out through all the earth,
    and their words to the end of the world.

In the heavens he has set a tent for the sun,
which comes out like a bridegroom from his wedding
    canopy,
    and like a strong man runs its course with joy.
Its rising is from the end of the heavens,
    and its circuit to the end of them;
    and nothing is hid from its heat.

The law of the LORD is perfect,
    reviving the soul;
the decrees of the LORD are sure,
    making wise the simple;

the precepts of the LORD are right,
    rejoicing the heart;
the commandment of the LORD is clear,
    enlightening the eyes;
the fear of the LORD is pure,
    enduring forever;
the ordinances of the LORD are true
    and righteous altogether.
More to be desired are they than gold,
    even much fine gold;
sweeter also than honey,
    and drippings of the honeycomb.

Moreover by them is your servant warned;
    in keeping them there is great reward.
But who can detect their errors?
    Clear me from hidden faults.
Keep back your servant also from the insolent;
    do not let them have dominion over me.
Then I shall be blameless,
    and innocent of great transgression.

Let the words of my mouth and the meditation of my heart
    be acceptable to you,
    O LORD, my rock and my redeemer.

Reflection

If you have been to a Black church worship service, you've likely heard Psalm 19 invoked. In many contexts, the concluding verses of this psalm, "Let the words of my mouth and the meditation of my heart be acceptable to you, O LORD, my rock and my redeemer," serve as a prayer of transition preparing the way for the preacher's sermon. This ritualized expression of our dependence on God is not just for clergy, but for all of us. What teacher, lawyer, social worker, or daycare provider feels exempt from the scope of this prayer? Every part of our life is filled with words, and our reliance upon language makes the message of this psalm constantly relevant. Our daily prayer, in whatever social setting we occupy, is that the words of our mouths and the meditations of our hearts find favor in God's sight.

Entrusting our thoughts and intentions to the Lord—to what contemplative theologian Howard Thurman calls the scrutiny of God's spirit—is simultaneously a humbling and empowering practice. Humbling because we desire God's acceptance of our speech. Empowering because the one from whom we seek approval is our Strength to both conceive thought and communicate it, our Redeemer to cleanse us when we need renewal.

The wider context of this psalm focuses on the meditations of God's heart, a precursor to the final focus on our own. This theme permeates the entire psalm. Everything from the heavenly bodies and the skies above to the instructions, decrees, and commands of the Lord, convey the glory, wisdom, and will of God to human beings. This essential point could not be more urgent or more relevant. As we ponder and put God's word in practice, we discover that the commandments of the Lord revive the soul, bring joy to the heart, *and* provide insight for living (v. 7-8). Be sure to move in both directions today, commending your innermost reflections and ideas to God, yes, but also studying and applying the binding, authoritative words of God within your own life.

Devotional

The psalmist contends that the heavens declare the glory of God. The beauty of creation is God's gift to us. Our stewardship and protection of this fragile creation is our response to God. When we savor the gift and cultivate it at the same time, we are practicing a justice imagination.

Set aside some time today to take a leisurely walk around where you live. As you stroll, let your heart drink deep from the beauty of creation and let your praise stream forth to our Maker, who fashioned the heavens and the earth.

Questions for the Day

- What does it look like for your very existence to bring glory to God? How are you already doing that now?
- Envision living in such a way that your daily rhythms speak of the glory of God without you ever even opening your mouth. What would that look like for you?
- Have you ever met anyone whose life embodied that kind of glory? What about their life spoke to you? How can you be inspired by them?

Let God Build It!

Psalm 127

Unless the LORD builds the house,
    those who build it labor in vain.
Unless the LORD guards the city,
    the guard keeps watch in vain.
It is in vain that you rise up early
    and go late to rest,
eating the bread of anxious toil;
    for he gives sleep to his beloved.

Sons are indeed a heritage from the LORD,
    the fruit of the womb a reward.
Like arrows in the hand of a warrior
    are the sons of one's youth.
Happy is the man who has
    his quiver full of them.
He shall not be put to shame
    when he speaks with his enemies in the gate.

Reflection

Psalm 127 is medicine for the anxious heart. With exquisite knowledge of the interior life, the psalmist declares in verse 2:

"It is in vain that you rise up early and go late to rest, eating the bread of anxious toil; for he gives sleep to his beloved." The phrase "anxious toil" highlights the hurried pace of labor that crowds out leisure, enjoyment, and a life of purpose. Our toil may come in the form of studying for school, handling our responsibilities at work, or reinventing our sense of vocation in retirement. Whatever the specifics, the enduring challenge of working without worrying, of laboring without becoming weary and heavy-laden, is a constant battle that ebbs and flows, but which we will never conquer this side of heaven. But we are not without hope! From Kirk Byron Jones to Barbara Holmes, Black contemplative Christians have maintained that immersion in the Spirit supplies the strength, laughter, and unspeakable joy needed to navigate each dimension of our lives.

This psalm also makes a political statement. Some jobs are anxious toil, not because the person doing the work needs an attitude adjustment, but because we participate in an economy that stratifies us based on our work. This economy provides status, legal protections, fair pay, and benefits to some kinds of work, but not to others. An oppressive society can exact a strong psychological toll on the downtrodden, but it cannot erase our autonomy. It cannot keep us from designing and discovering a life of significance, meaning, and impact.

Yet we must also confess that we cannot build a truly worthwhile life without centering our labor in the Lord. Verse 1 hammers this home, saying, "Unless the LORD builds the house, those who build it labor in vain. Unless the LORD guards the city, the guard keeps watch in vain." What an enduring idea! Unless the Lord raises the family, unless the Lord upholds the church, unless the Lord continues to strengthen the Black freedom struggle, the victories lose some of their luster and the losses take on more weight. Let today be a day when you resolve to build and labor alongside our God, in whom all our labor—even our failures—find their place and purpose.

Devotional

God grants rest to her beloved. This is what the psalmist tells us. Take your rest this evening as an act of spiritual resistance within a capitalist culture that idolizes professional achievement and workplace effort. Deep rest, not merely bodily recuperation, but physical, emotional, and spiritual restoration, is an embodied practice that strengthens our justice imagination.

By embracing your rest, without guilt or anxiety, you experience divine grace, a foretaste of sabbath rest in the world to come. This evening, take your rest, child of God. You deserve it.

Questions for the Day

- What have you seen God build? What does this tell you about God?
- What do you need God to build? How can you work alongside God to make the visions of your justice imaginationan a reality?
- What have you built without God that you saw crumble? How could God help you rebuild it or build something better in its place?

Praying through Depression

Psalm 116 (NLT)

I love the LORD because he hears my voice
    and my prayer for mercy.
Because he bends down to listen,
    I will pray as long as I have breath!
Death wrapped its ropes around me;
    the terrors of the grave overtook me.
    I saw only trouble and sorrow.
Then I called on the name of the LORD:
    "Please, LORD, save me!"
How kind the LORD is! How good he is!
    So merciful, this God of ours!
The LORD protects those of childlike faith;
    I was facing death, and he saved me.
Let my soul be at rest again,
    for the LORD has been good to me.
He has saved me from death,
    my eyes from tears,
    my feet from stumbling.
And so I walk in the LORD's presence
    as I live here on earth!

I believed in you, so I said,
   "I am deeply troubled, LORD."
In my anxiety I cried out to you,
   "These people are all liars!"
What can I offer the LORD
   for all he has done for me?
I will lift up the cup of salvation
   and praise the LORD's name for saving me.
I will keep my promises to the LORD
   in the presence of all his people.

The LORD cares deeply
   when his loved ones die.
O LORD, I am your servant;
   yes, I am your servant, born into your household;
   you have freed me from my chains.
I will offer you a sacrifice of thanksgiving
   and call on the name of the LORD.
I will fulfill my vows to the LORD
   in the presence of all his people—
in the house of the LORD
   in the heart of Jerusalem.

Praise the LORD!

Reflection

"I love the Lord, who heard my cry and pitied every groan.
Long as I live and troubles rise, I'll hasten to God's throne."
These memorable lyrics, sung in Black congregations across
the country and immortalized by Whitney Houston in *The*

Preacher's Wife, are inspired by the opening verses of today's psalm. Verses 1-2 read, "I love the Lord because he hears my voice and my prayer for mercy. Because he bends down to listen, I will pray as long as I have breath."

These verses call on us to recognize the multitude of reasons we have to love the Lord. We don't just love the Lord out of instinct. Instead, according to the psalmist, our love for God is justified because God is the one who hears our voice and our pleas. Most intimately of all, God is the one who "bends down to listen." God answers our prayers and angles down from the divine throne to hear all our problems and petitions. This psalm provides us with an image of a God who is always present, always before us. It's an image of a God who is close enough to hear our private concerns, but also powerful enough to protect us and deal bountifully with us (v. 6-7). These verses helps us understand that we love God because we ourselves are cared for, preserved, and listened to by an awesome, accommodating, and mighty God. Within our hearts should not just be a vague affinity for God, but an informed feeling of trust and a sense of reliance on our Creator, Maker, and Deliverer.

These are difficult times for Black lives. Having barely recovered from the Great Recession, we were then struck by the brute force of COVID-19, a resulting economic crisis, and hypervisible police violence. Some of us have had to repeat along with the psalmist the words of verse 15, "The LORD cares deeply when his loved ones die." Despite these difficult experiences, it remains true that life is not perpetually the story of death, doom, and disaster. There is also, according to the psalmist, deliverance. Verse 8 celebrates that God has, "saved me from death, my eyes from tears, my feet from stumbling." Whether deliverance is entire or partial, immediate or prolonged, psychological or social, God is a deliverer. Secure in that conviction, let us maintain a roughhewn confidence that can say, "I believed in you, so I said, 'I am deeply troubled, LORD.'" (v. 10).

Devotional

The psalmist connects the love of God to God's capacity for empathy, specifically how the Lord pities our groans and hears our cries. What traumas, what long-endured wounds, has God heard groaning within you? Within your community? Living from the conviction that God hears us and moves to put right the various sources of our spiritual, social, and psychological pain is an essential thread of a justice imagination.

The experience of being understood, seen, and cared for forms the foundation of our love for a God who, in the words of the well-known song, "will hear our faintest cry" and "answer by and by."

"Stand ten toes down" is a saying that young people sometimes use. It's a way of saying that people should stand firm, digging their toes in the ground to ensure that they do not waver. So we say to you, stand ten toes down in these experiences. They constitute a basis of our innermost attachment to our triune God.

Questions for the Day

- Depression is real. We all have times in our lives where we feel as the psalmist did in this passage. It's important to know that sorrow occurs in life. It makes you no less

Christian to have to battle sorrow. How have you experienced depression in your life? How can you take comfort in the words of the psalmist?

- We all need to whisper the prayer, "Lord, save me," every now and again. What do these words mean to you?
- Envision a world where your sorrow isn't a signal that you have done something wrong, but rather a response to the circumstances of life that come despite our best attempts to avoid them. What does this world look like? How can you live in this world? How can you help others live here?
- The Lord has been good to you. Rest is a gift from God. What does it look like for you to rest today?

Deliver Us from Our Enemies

Psalm 83

O God, do not keep silence;
    do not hold your peace or be still, O God!
Even now your enemies are in tumult;
    those who hate you have raised their heads.
They lay crafty plans against your people;
    they consult together against those you protect.
They say, "Come, let us wipe them out as a nation;
    let the name of Israel be remembered no more."
They conspire with one accord;
    against you they make a covenant—
the tents of Edom and the Ishmaelites,
    Moab and the Hagrites,
Gebal and Ammon and Amalek,
    Philistia with the inhabitants of Tyre;
Assyria also has joined them;
    they are the strong arm of the children of Lot.   *Selah*

Do to them as you did to Midian,
    as to Sisera and Jabin at the Wadi Kishon,
who were destroyed at En-dor,
    who became dung for the ground.

Make their nobles like Oreb and Zeeb,
    all their princes like Zebah and Zalmunna,
who said, "Let us take the pastures of God
    for our own possession."

O my God, make them like whirling dust,
    like chaff before the wind.
As fire consumes the forest,
    as the flame sets the mountains ablaze,
so pursue them with your tempest
    and terrify them with your hurricane.
Fill their faces with shame,
    so that they may seek your name, O LORD.
Let them be put to shame and dismayed forever;
    let them perish in disgrace.
Let them know that you alone,
    whose name is the LORD,
    are the Most High over all the earth.

Reflection

The Psalms talk about enemies. Not haters. Not naysayers. Enemies. The Psalms acknowledge that walking with God means encountering enemies who will threaten, belittle, scoff, kill, and otherwise harm God's people. Our lived experience includes enemies of all sorts. An economy that works for the wealthy few at the expense of the poor is an enemy. A society that values men more than women is an enemy. These structures and more are the tools of the accuser—that is, Satan—who is seeking to destroy us.

Psalm 83 speaks to our faith journey from within this matrix of enemies and calls for us to trust in divine deliverance. Its opening invocation sets the stage, "O God, do not keep silence; do not hold your peace or be still, O God!" Facing enemies is hard enough—facing enemies with a silent God is unbearable. The plea of verse 1 captures the blend of thoughts, feelings, and premonitions we experience when we are fighting for our lives. Such moments call forth unusual prayers. They bring out blunt calls for help, not decorated petitions. As long as the scourges of police violence, community violence, and intimate partner violence are injuring our people, we must urge God to speak through sermons, through prayer, through laws and regulations, and through cultural consensus that prioritizes nonviolence and peace. The words of our prayer are simple, the implications plain, and their audience clear: God, break the silence and move against our enemies with the weightiness of your nonviolent peace.

Giving ourselves permission to keep our prayer talk plain and welcoming blunt calls for help against our enemies promotes honest *and* healing communication with God in both directions. Picturesque prayers have their place, of course. God remains an unseen presence who can only be described using images and language that partly, but never entirely, capture the divine essence. But we must admit that a major spiritual enemy we struggle to overcome is the impulse to be buttoned up, sobered up, and filled with religious jargon when we pray. This is nonsense! Nothing could be more false! Jesus tells us to worship the God who parents us all, in spirit and in truth—surely, a call for candid, unpretentious prayer

(John 4:24). God accepts and desires our prayers to come from a simple, real place, and not an inauthentic or manufactured one.

This kind of simple prayer, the undisguised urge of hearts stretching toward heaven, is a prompt calling God to handle our enemies, both real and imagined, external and internal. In verse 18, the psalmist makes a bold request for God to act with our enemies in full view. He calls on God to, "Let them know that you alone, whose name is the LORD, are the Most High over all the earth." Remember and rejoice in this relational reality. The Most High is above all enemies, and in due time, will make them our footstool. Be humble, however, for the equality and power of God thwarts the "crafty plans" of all oppressors—including both the plans of those who seek to dominate us and, at times, our own oppressive plans as well.

Devotional

God promises to deliver us from enemies. This promise is a recurring theme in prayer lives shaped by the Psalter and a justice imagination.

Reserve time today to pray the following words about our collective enemies: "Gracious God of Liberation, free us from our enemies. And when we are the enemies, transform us from oppressing others into removing the yoke from their necks and practicing freedom. In Christ's name, Amen."

Questions for the Day

- Are some things off limits in prayer? The psalmist is pretty clear here about how he wants God to handle his enemies. He holds nothing back. How can you practice honestly naming what you want God to do?

- What does it mean to you to know that the Holy Spirit will interpret everything your heart and soul longs to say even when you can't find the words? How can this change the way you pray?
- Though the psalmist wishes nothing good for his enemies, I wonder if we can move beyond that state and imagine good things even for those who aren't for us. What would it look like to have the capacity to both desire that folks are taught a lesson not to mess with God's people and for those folks to come into the awareness that God loves them too? What might redemption look like?
- If you were to re-write the last few verses of this psalm in a way that offers redemption for your enemies, what would you say?

Lord, You Know Me

Psalm 139

O Lord, you have searched me and known me.
You know when I sit down and when I rise up;
   you discern my thoughts from far away.
You search out my path and my lying down,
   and are acquainted with all my ways.
Even before a word is on my tongue,
   O Lord, you know it completely.
You hem me in, behind and before,
   and lay your hand upon me.
Such knowledge is too wonderful for me;
   it is so high that I cannot attain it.

Where can I go from your spirit?
   Or where can I flee from your presence?
If I ascend to heaven, you are there;
   if I make my bed in Sheol, you are there.
If I take the wings of the morning
   and settle at the farthest limits of the sea,
even there your hand shall lead me,
   and your right hand shall hold me fast.
If I say, "Surely the darkness shall cover me,
   and the light around me become night,"

even the darkness is not dark to you;
    the night is as bright as the day,
    for darkness is as light to you.

For it was you who formed my inward parts;
    you knit me together in my mother's womb.
I praise you, for I am fearfully and wonderfully made.
    Wonderful are your works;
that I know very well.
    My frame was not hidden from you,
when I was being made in secret,
    intricately woven in the depths of the earth.
Your eyes beheld my unformed substance.
In your book were written
    all the days that were formed for me,
    when none of them as yet existed.
How weighty to me are your thoughts, O God!
    How vast is the sum of them!
I try to count them—they are more than the sand;
    I come to the end—I am still with you.

O that you would kill the wicked, O God,
    and that the bloodthirsty would depart from me—
those who speak of you maliciously,
    and lift themselves up against you for evil!
Do I not hate those who hate you, O LORD?
    And do I not loathe those who rise up against you?
I hate them with perfect hatred;
    I count them my enemies.
Search me, O God, and know my heart;
    test me and know my thoughts.

See if there is any wicked way in me,
    and lead me in the way everlasting.

Reflection

God is everywhere. Psalm 139:7-12 testifies that God always keeps company with human beings. God is always present, but we can go further because God's presence is not a dry, static reality. God's presence is not like the air, which is always around us but easy to forget. Rather, God's presence is like a mother who is always a text message away and who sometimes calls us without prompting. God is like a Black grandmother on an ever-expanding front porch, calling us to come home and to have a little talk to sort out life. Like that grandmother, God is always welcoming us, mindful of us, and loving toward us, which, yes, sometimes means correcting us and confronting us.

The psalmist claims that God enjoys a unique, psychological relationship with each of us. The opening verses bear witness to this with the psalmist declaring that God searches us and knows us intimately, that God knows us so well that God knows when we sit down and when we get up. Furthermore, the psalmist notes that before a word is formed on our lips, God knows it. Where else could this relationship be held but within our hearts, spirits, and minds?

Our connection with God also depends on our faith community, which equips us with a canon of symbols, stories, and confessions about God. This language and these traditions of biblical revelation provide us with the tools we need to recognize that God is with us and to express that conviction to the world. This conviction, this knowledge that God is not only with us but knows us intimately evokes wonder and leaves us to marvel at God's majesty. In fact, God knows us better than anyone else, including ourselves. In verse 6, the psalmist responds to this realization that God knows everything about him, saying, "Such knowledge is too wonderful for me; it is so high that I cannot attain it." This sentiment is echoed again in verse 17, "How weighty to me are your thoughts, O God! How vast is the sum of them!"

How should we respond to this revelation about God's knowledge of our bodies, our thoughts, and our whereabouts? By giving ourselves over to God's disarming judgment, offering our lives to God, and following God's lead. In the concluding words of the psalmist, "Search me, O God, and know my heart; test me and know my thoughts. See if there is any wicked way in me, and lead me in the way everlasting" (v. 23-24).

Devotional

Today's psalm invites us to slow down and yield ourselves to divine examination. Prayers of examination orient our justice imagination toward teachability and genuine righteousness, rather than self-righteousness. Claim the concluding verses of this psalm as your own. Focus, in particular, on the action words.

After reading the psalm, offer the following words to God from your heart, "Merciful God, before whom everything is known, and nothing is hidden, search me, know me, test me, then lead me. For the good of creation, for the betterment of Black people, for my own life, may it be so, in Jesus' name."

Questions for the Day

- Have you ever been afraid to let someone know the real you because you think that person will not accept you? We can take courage in knowing that God knows our innermost parts and loves us still. Write down a few things about yourself that you hide from those you love.
- Now ask yourself, "Why do I hide these things? Are these things wicked?"
- Remind yourself that God can expose any wicked tendencies within us and help us get rid of those pieces of ourselves that mean others harm. You are not doomed. You can recover. God is ready to help you live the kind of life that you can be proud of sharing with those you love. Let God search you.

The Lord, Our Protector

Psalm 16

Protect me, O God, for in you I take refuge.
I say to the LORD, "You are my Lord;
  I have no good apart from you."

As for the holy ones in the land, they are the noble,
  in whom is all my delight.

Those who choose another god multiply their sorrows;
  their drink offerings of blood I will not pour out
  or take their names upon my lips.

The LORD is my chosen portion and my cup;
  you hold my lot.
The boundary lines have fallen for me in pleasant places;
  I have a goodly heritage.

I bless the LORD who gives me counsel;
  in the night also my heart instructs me.
I keep the LORD always before me;
  because he is at my right hand, I shall not be moved.

Therefore my heart is glad, and my soul rejoices;
  my body also rests secure.

For you do not give me up to Sheol,
    or let your faithful one see the Pit.

You show me the path of life.
    In your presence there is fullness of joy;
    in your right hand are pleasures forevermore.

Reflection

The psalmist calls us to connect our praise to divine guidance. Consider verses 7-8, where the psalmist says, "I bless the LORD who gives me counsel; in the night also my heart instructs me. I keep the LORD always before me; because he is at my right hand, I shall not be moved." In these verses, we are encouraged to praise God alongside a nod to the importance of God's guidance. The implication here is that we praise God because God instructs our hearts—so much so, in fact, that nighttime is also instructional time for the Spirit. God leads us from timidity to courage, from second-guessing ourselves to drawing strength from heaven. From dawn to dusk, the guidance we receive from God leads us to choose wisdom, justice, and love in our lived experiences.

Psalm 16 also testifies to the ways we find our protection and safety in God. Verses 1 and 9 capture this confession well. In verse 1, the psalmist opens, "Protect me, O God, for in you I take refuge," and in verse 9, he proclaims, "Therefore my heart is glad, and my soul rejoices; my body also rests secure." Interpreted together, these verses link our potential for gladness and joy to a multifaceted sense of safety. Notice that the theme of refuge in verse 1 appears again in verse 9 in the words, "My body also rests secure." This embodied sense of physical safety, paired with a spiritual and psychological sense of refuge, resonates with the complex realities of Black life.

We need safety. We need peace. We need the peace of God that Paul describes in Philippians 4:7, saying it "surpasses all understanding" and that it "will guard your hearts and your minds in Christ Jesus." We need the peace of God found in the word *shalom,* an encompassing harmony between human communities, spiritual powers, ecosystems, and social structures that reflects God's desire and intention for the world. In a society that wars against and welts Black flesh, stand in the dignity of verse 9 by claiming that your body deserves to "rest secure"—not eviction, not police violence, not intimate partner harm. As we tilt toward these realities, may we savor and revel, with the psalmist, in the joy of divine presence and the pleasures of moments lived with God.

Devotional

This psalm encourages us to demand peace and genuine public safety, both for ourselves and for others. Practicing a justice imagination with regard to public safety isn't about supporting the troops or getting more cops on the street. Rather, practicing a justice imagination is about making and demanding peace, and allowing a community response—including mental health professionals, movement chaplains, neighborhood residents, and social workers—to lead the charge.

As you ponder what the Spirit is saying through this passage, claim God's guidance for yourself, not from the viewpoint of your imagined future, *but from where you are now.* Name the refuge of God as your own—as belonging to you, your family, and to all Black diasporic people.

Questions for the Day

- Do you realize that God created you? Have you paused recently to sit with the fact that God shaped you and knows the innermost parts of you?
- How can you practice slowing down long enough to be attentive to your innermost parts? Who are you in your innermost parts?
- What do you think God whispered to your soul as God fashioned you in your mother's womb? Who would God say you are?

The God Our Ancestors Told Us About

Psalm 44

We have heard with our ears, O God,
  our ancestors have told us,
what deeds you performed in their days,
  in the days of old:
you with your own hand drove out the nations,
  but them you planted;
you afflicted the peoples,
  but them you set free;
for not by their own sword did they win the land,
  nor did their own arm give them victory;
but your right hand, and your arm,
  and the light of your countenance,
  for you delighted in them.

You are my King and my God;
  you command victories for Jacob.
Through you we push down our foes;
  through your name we tread down our assailants.
For not in my bow do I trust,
  nor can my sword save me.
But you have saved us from our foes,
  and have put to confusion those who hate us.

In God we have boasted continually,
    and we will give thanks to your name forever.   *Selah*

Yet you have rejected us and abased us,
    and have not gone out with our armies.
You made us turn back from the foe,
    and our enemies have gotten spoil.
You have made us like sheep for slaughter,
    and have scattered us among the nations.
You have sold your people for a trifle,
    demanding no high price for them.

You have made us the taunt of our neighbors,
    the derision and scorn of those around us.
You have made us a byword among the nations,
    a laughingstock among the peoples.
All day long my disgrace is before me,
    and shame has covered my face
at the words of the taunters and revilers,
    at the sight of the enemy and the avenger.

All this has come upon us,
    yet we have not forgotten you,
    or been false to your covenant.
Our heart has not turned back,
    nor have our steps departed from your way,
yet you have broken us in the haunt of jackals,
    and covered us with deep darkness.

If we had forgotten the name of our God,
    or spread out our hands to a strange god,
would not God discover this?
    For he knows the secrets of the heart.

Because of you we are being killed all day long,
  and accounted as sheep for the slaughter.

Rouse yourself! Why do you sleep, O Lord?
  Awake, do not cast us off forever!
Why do you hide your face?
  Why do you forget our affliction and oppression?
For we sink down to the dust;
  our bodies cling to the ground.
Rise up, come to our help.
  Redeem us for the sake of your steadfast love.

Reflection

Ancestors are connectors. They unfold a bridge toward us, connecting our faltering belief to a more ancient faith, granting access to a tradition wider than our own interests, and rooting us in identities stronger than the powers and principalities seeking to crush us. Black Christian ancestors, in the language of Hebrews 11, are a cloud of witnesses encouraging and correcting us. Whether these ancestors come from within our family tree, our intimate circles, or whether they're famous ancestors of faith—the Harriet Tubmans, the Martin Luther Kings, and so on—their faith is meant not to transfix us in admiration, but rather to spark transformative faith that spurs us to action.

Our psalmist, in verses 1-2 articulates a deep commitment to the ancestors of his community, saying, "We have heard with our ears, O God, *our ancestors have told us,* what deeds you performed in their days, in the days of old: you with your own hand drove out the nations, *but them you planted*; you afflicted the peoples, *but them you set free*" (emphasis added).

Who are your ancestors? What are they trying to tell you about what God performed "in their days"? How might we learn and grow in our understanding of how the Lord set our ancestors free? Our understanding of the role of ancestors in strengthening the faith of Black diasporic culture is also rooted in this psalm. Let your forebears call you toward greater works in Christ and a greater sense of peace. Let them inspire you to defy every pressure and evil aligned against you.

Devotional

The African tradition of libation is a spiritual practice of honoring ancestors. Celebrating those who have gone before us ensures that our justice imagination is historically grounded and indebted to the cloud of witnesses whose works and presence still encourage us today.

Libation consists of pouring out a cup of water into a plant, or even on the ground, to express honor and remembrance of our forebears. Inspired by that practice and this psalm, set aside five minutes to conduct a libation for your ancestors. Fill a cup of water and slowly pour out the cup in successive tilts. With each tilt, speak the name of an ancestor whose life, faith, and witness encourage you. Do this until you have called the name of at least five ancestors, thanking God for their lives and legacy.

Questions for the Day

- What ancestors have you placed on metaphorical pedestals? What historical figures seem larger than life to you? Who are the folks you think of when you tell yourself, "I could never do that!"?
- How can you turn that awe of your ancestors into action? How can you move from admiration to inspiration?
- Write down the names of the ancestors you wish to honor as you move through life. For whom do you pour out your libation?

You Deserve to Be Happy

Psalm 84

How lovely is your dwelling place,
    O LORD of hosts!
My soul longs, indeed it faints
    for the courts of the LORD;
my heart and my flesh sing for joy
    to the living God.

Even the sparrow finds a home,
    and the swallow a nest for herself,
    where she may lay her young,
at your altars, O LORD of hosts,
my King and my God.
Happy are those who live in your house,
    ever singing your praise.   *Selah*

Happy are those whose strength is in you,
    in whose heart are the highways to Zion.
As they go through the valley of Baca
    they make it a place of springs;
    the early rain also covers it with pools.
They go from strength to strength;
the God of gods will be seen in Zion.

O Lord God of hosts, hear my prayer;
 give ear, O God of Jacob!   *Selah*
Behold our shield, O God;
 look on the face of your anointed.

For a day in your courts is better
 than a thousand elsewhere.
I would rather be a doorkeeper in the house of my God
 than live in the tents of wickedness.
For the Lord God is a sun and shield;
 he bestows favor and honor.
No good thing does the Lord withhold
 from those who walk uprightly.
O Lord of hosts,
 happy is everyone who trusts in you.

Reflection

There really is nothing like the Black church experience. There's a reason why so many R&B singers got their start in the church. There's a reason why so many politicians and public speakers learned their confidence in the Black church. Much of the Black community has found some form of training within the four walls of their local church.

Yet, the COVID-19 pandemic has caused us to reconsider what it means to be the church outside the confines of the building. In the days of social distancing and quarantine, many of us found ourselves longing, like the psalmist, for an opportunity to be in the tabernacle of our God.

It was in the beginning days of the COVID-19 pandemic that the words of Psalm 84 came to life for me. Suddenly, I too longed for a day in the courts of my God. I yearned to gather with the believers, the fellowship of the saints. I craved the laughter of the children and the wisdom of the elderly. I simply missed being in communion with the body of Christ.

While in the midst of that somber solitude, Psalm 84 resonated differently. I realized that when the psalmist wrote these words, the only access he had to God was within the walls of the physical tabernacle. In that time, the only way he could visit with God was to go to the physical location where the Spirit of the Lord resided. But now, because of the sacrifice of Jesus Christ, we can access the presence of the Lord wherever we are. We can enter the courts of our God from our homes, in our cars, in the grocery store, at the barber shop—wherever we are, whenever we need, we now have the privilege of spending time in God's presence.

Despite this, many of us still experience the presence of God only within the four walls of the church. This happens when we do not create an atmosphere of worship and praise in our homes. Too often, we wait for the melodic voices of our church choirs, the funky melodies of our church bands, and the convicting messages of our clergy to help us connect with God. But Psalm 84 reflects not only a longing to go within the four walls of the church, but also a longing to be in God's presence all the time, wherever that might be.

Devotional

Today, we encourage you to look for God's presence somewhere other than a physical church building. Embodying a justice imagination expands our geography of where God is present beyond the sanctuary and calls us to believe that the earth is the Lord's and that God can and will meet us anywhere.

Starting today, be on the lookout for God's presence in music. Thirst for God's presence in nature. Search for God's presence both in the stillness of your heart and in the noisiness of protest movements for Black lives. When you find it, cherish it. Linger in it. Allow it to shape you into the person you are becoming. Search for it every day.

Questions for the Day

- Everybody wants to be happy. How do you define happiness?
- This passage tells us that happiness comes to those who spend time in the Lord's presence and who trust in the Lord. How is your trust these days? On a scale of one to ten, where do you fall?
- You deserve to be happy. No good thing will the Lord withhold. Go after your happiness.

What If?

Psalm 124 (NLT)

What if the LORD had not been on our side?
   Let all Israel repeat:
What if the LORD had not been on our side
   when people attacked us?
They would have swallowed us alive
   in their burning anger.
The waters would have engulfed us;
   a torrent would have overwhelmed us.
Yes, the raging waters of their fury
   would have overwhelmed our very lives.

Praise the LORD,
   who did not let their teeth tear us apart!
We escaped like a bird from a hunter's trap.
   The trap is broken, and we are free!
Our help is from the LORD,
   who made heaven and earth.

Reflection

If it had not been! We can pause and shout right there. As Black lives in America, we know a thing or two about our enemies seeking to snuff out our lives. Our people know what it's like to be hunted, brutalized, feared, and discarded, yet we continue to blossom, flourish, and thrive. How? Because the Lord has been on our side.

Now, for many that sentence doesn't compute. I can hear you asking, "How could the Lord be on the side of Black folks when Black folks have been brutalized for so long? How could the Lord be on the side of Black folks who have had, in too many instances, to fend for themselves?"

I say to you, the Lord has been on the side of Black folks because the Lord is on the side of the oppressed. God hates injustice. God is on the side of the marginalized. God is on the side of those whose backs are against the wall, as Howard Thurman would say. Yet God has granted human beings free will and agency to make their own decisions. Regrettably, people have allowed their greed and selfish ambition to run amok. This has led them to enslave and brutalize those they feel are inferior to them. People in power make choices every day about how they will engage those who have less power than they do. In America, historically, white men have held the dominant forms of power, exerting their will over every other demographic. White women have followed as the second most powerful demographic within the United States of America.

Yet Black people in America continue to rise above the limitations that those in power place upon us. Just as Psalm 124 proclaims that God helped the people of Israel keep their head above water, preserve their souls, escape the traps of their enemies, and live to tell the story, so it is with Black

Americans. Though the systems enslaved our bodies, they could not enslave our minds. Though the systems segregated our bodies, they could not segregate our souls.

If it had not been for the Lord on our side, we wouldn't have made it out of chattel slavery. If it had not been for the Lord on our side, we wouldn't have been able to build a life for ourselves without our forty acres and a mule. If it had not been for the Lord on our side, we wouldn't have been able to overturn Jim Crow laws and desegregate this nation. If it had not been for the Lord on our side, we wouldn't have been able to occupy professions that were previously designated for whites only. If it had not been for the Lord on our side, where would we be?

The psalmist doesn't forget the trouble his people endured, but he remembers that God made a way out. As you meditate today, meditate on the ways that God has made for you to escape. Think about the battles God has fought for you. Think about the doors God has opened *and* the doors God has shut. Think about the times that you couldn't see your way out, but God stepped in. Think about the things that your enemies meant for evil that God turned around for your good.

If it had not been for the Lord on our side, where would we be?

Devotional

The survival of Black people in the Americas, given the horrors of the transatlantic slave trade, convict leasing, lynching, sharecropping, Jim Crow, and mass incarceration, is a miracle. Some consider that history and worry, "Where was

God?" A fair question, but in today's devotional, let's instead wonder, "Who else but God?" Who else but God could sustain a diasporic people enduring such collective harm? Cultivating the capacity to wonder, to ask old questions in new ways, is to think with a justice imagination.

This psalm invites us to wonder instead of worry. Considering yourself, wonder and wander through your memory. What miracles of preservation has God done in your life? Where has God done a mighty work in your world? The social and material basis of worry is real, but so is our spiritual agency to choose wonder over worry and astonishment over anguish.

Questions for the Day

- Practice a spirit of gratitude that remembers what you've been through. Holy memory helps us to know that we didn't get where we are by ourselves. What does holy memory mean to you?

- How has God shown up in your life over the years? How can you make it a practice to thank God for what God has done?

- Sometimes we forget all the things God has protected us from, delivered us from, restored us to. God is a merciful God whose faithfulness is everlasting. We owe God our gratitude. We owe God our memory! What memories do you have about God protecting you? How has God protected your community? Your ancestors?

God Cares

Psalm 23 (NLT)

The LORD is my shepherd;
    I have all that I need.
He lets me rest in green meadows;
    he leads me beside peaceful streams.
    He renews my strength.
He guides me along right paths,
    bringing honor to his name.
Even when I walk
    through the darkest valley,
I will not be afraid,
    for you are close beside me.
Your rod and your staff
    protect and comfort me.
You prepare a feast for me
    in the presence of my enemies.
You honor me by anointing my head with oil.
    My cup overflows with blessings.
Surely your goodness and unfailing love will pursue me
    all the days of my life,
and I will live in the house of the LORD
    forever.

Reflection

Psalm 23 is a psalm of care. It reminds us that God cares for us and that God will always take care of us. This psalm tells us that God will grant us rest (v. 2), peace (v. 2), renewal (v. 3), guidance (v. 3), companionship (v. 4), sustenance (v. 5), honor (v. 5), protection (v. 5), abundance (v. 5), goodness (v. 6), love (v. 6), longevity (v. 6), and access to God's presence (v. 6).

What a gift! What a sigh of relief to know that God is caring for us and we can rest in God's presence. Often, as we settle into adulthood, we become accustomed to caring for everyone else. Only rarely do we have someone caring for us. Psalm 23 reminds us that God is up to good things in our lives. God cares. As a shepherd cares for their sheep, so God cares for us.

If you've found yourself feeling as though no one cares about you, remember this psalm. God cares and is actively working to grant you rest, peace, renewal, guidance, companionship, sustenance, honor, protection, abundance, goodness, love, longevity, and access to God's presence. God is working to ensure that you shall not want for these things. God's got it covered. Trust the shepherd.

Devotional

Trusting God to shepherd us sometimes means naming the barriers to our trust. Cultivating our reliance on God may not appear to be part of developing a justice imagination, but it's essential. By building our trust in the Lord, we ensure that our justice work emerges from an intimate union with God rather than from a place of alienation.

Set aside twenty minutes today to write a journal entry about trust. During that time, write down your trust barriers, the experiences, beliefs, or circumstances that make trusting God challenging. Then, take your trust barriers to the altar, writing out a prayer like this, "God of grace and mercy, unearth the root causes that make it hard for me to trust; help me to rely on you, follow you, and honor you. Be my shepherd, guide, and protection, in Christ's name. Amen."

Questions for the Day

- On the first day of class, my divinity school professor, Dr. Frederick Streets, asked us, "What if God prepared a table before you in the presence of your enemies so that your enemies could eat too?" What would this look like in your context?
- What would happen if God decided to take care of you and provide for your enemies? Are you mature enough to still thank God for your protection and your provision?
- How can you practice not needing others to suffer in order for you to feel like you're thriving? What does it look like for God to care for each of us in our own unique ways? What does it look like when we all get to eat?

A Prayer When Your Eyes Are Full of Tears

Psalm 88 (NLT)

O LORD, God of my salvation,
    I cry out to you by day.
    I come to you at night.
Now hear my prayer;
    listen to my cry.
For my life is full of troubles,
    and death draws near.
I am as good as dead,
    like a strong man with no strength left.
They have left me among the dead,
    and I lie like a corpse in a grave.
I am forgotten,
    cut off from your care.
You have thrown me into the lowest pit,
    into the darkest depths.
Your anger weighs me down;
    with wave after wave you have engulfed me.   *Interlude*

You have driven my friends away
by making me repulsive to them.
I am in a trap with no way of escape.
    My eyes are blinded by my tears.

Each day I beg for your help, O LORD;
   I lift my hands to you for mercy.
Are your wonderful deeds of any use to the dead?
Do the dead rise up and praise you?   *Interlude*

Can those in the grave declare your unfailing love?
   Can they proclaim your faithfulness in the place of
   destruction?
Can the darkness speak of your wonderful deeds?
   Can anyone in the land of forgetfulness talk about your
   righteousness?
O LORD, I cry out to you.
   I will keep on pleading day by day.
O LORD, why do you reject me?
   Why do you turn your face from me?

I have been sick and close to death since my youth.
   I stand helpless and desperate before your terrors.
Your fierce anger has overwhelmed me.
   Your terrors have paralyzed me.
They swirl around me like floodwaters all day long.
They have engulfed me completely.
You have taken away my companions and loved ones.
   Darkness is my closest friend.

Reflection

There are some days when our prayers don't offer a silver lining. There are times when life has taken its course and all we have left are our tears. In today's psalm, the psalmist feels isolated and abandoned. He feels near death and without much hope. He's calling out to God, seemingly receiving no answer. As a result, he's angry with God. He doesn't know why God isn't answering him.

Have you ever been there? Have you ever gotten to a place of desperation and pleading with God? That's where the psalmist is here. He's got nothing left.

But the powerful thing is that he is *still* calling upon God. He doesn't let the lack of response keep him from going to God in prayer.

Sometimes prayer is the last thing you want to do, but also the thing that you most need to do. Put simply, prayer is a conversation with God. When life starts to fall apart, you need to be able to name what is happening to you. And when you name it, when you say it aloud to God, you show that you still have hope. That's the beauty of prayer. When you pray, you're showing God that you have hope that God will answer and respond to you.

Verses 1-2 say, "O LORD, God of my salvation, I cry out to you by day. I come to you at night. Now hear my prayer; listen to my cry." This is the prayer of someone who still has hope. He is despondent. He is at his wits' end and likely at a breaking point, but the language of prayer pushes him toward hope.

Prayer forces us to confront the situations we are in and the changes that we need. Prayer keeps us honest. Prayer also keeps us aware and attuned to the things that are happening in our lives.

Everybody gets to a low place like this where they can't find God. That solidarity is the encouragement that the psalmist offers. If you're in that kind of place right now, keep praying. Keep being honest with yourself about where you are and what you need. As you cry out to God, you're also reminding your soul of what you need. Through prayer, we gain perspective. Through prayer, we gain patience. Through prayer, we gain intimacy with God.

If you're in a moment of your life where this psalm captures the sentiments of your heart, you are in good company. All who have walked with God have felt this way at some point. But God is a faithful God. God always keeps the promises God makes. While you might be in a Psalm 88 season in your life, know that seasons change, and this one will too. It won't always be like this. Keep talking to God about your situation because at some point God is going to speak. At some point, God will respond. Let this psalm remind you that everyone goes through trials. Everyone has low moments of uncertainty and fear, but God is a loving God. That love transcends everything else and will keep you, even when you don't want to be kept, even when you feel that you don't deserve it.

Devotional

Our prayer is that you feel God's love today. Close your eyes; visualize the love of God covering your face like a morning mist or a gentle rainfall. For just a few moments, envision God's love holding you, enfolding you in a warm embrace.

When our love comes from a deeply felt belief that we are God's beloved, we love our neighbors, strangers, and even our enemies from a justice imagination big enough to encompass the sorrow, anguish, and unresolved pain that accompanies holistic faith.

May you, and everyone connected to you, experience unfiltered, divine love today. As you navigate these Psalm 88 moments, our prayer on your behalf is that God will incline God's ear toward you. We are praying with you, believing with you, that whatever you're experiencing will be turned around in due time, both for your good personally, and for our good as a people.

Questions for the Day

- When is the last time you felt low like this? How did you cope? How did you recover?
- This psalm gives attention to the fact that sometimes we are simply overcome with despair. This psalm is uncomfortable. It doesn't offer silver linings. It forces us to sit with the pain. When is the last time you gave yourself permission to sit with the pain?
- Your pain is a reminder that things have got to change. Whenever you ignore your pain, you delay your change. How can you feel your pain without being afraid of it? What can our pain teach us? What can it say to us that we need to hear?

I Am Confident!

Psalm 108 (NLT)

My heart is confident in you, O God;
> no wonder I can sing your praises with all my heart!

Wake up, lyre and harp!
> I will wake the dawn with my song.

I will thank you, LORD, among all the people.
> I will sing your praises among the nations.

For your unfailing love is higher than the heavens.
> Your faithfulness reaches to the clouds.

Be exalted, O God, above the highest heavens.
> May your glory shine over all the earth.

Now rescue your beloved people.
> Answer and save us by your power.

God has promised this by his holiness:
"I will divide up Shechem with joy.
> I will measure out the valley of Succoth.

Gilead is mine,
> and Manasseh, too.

Ephraim, my helmet, will produce my warriors,
> and Judah, my scepter, will produce my kings.

But Moab, my washbasin, will become my servant,
    and I will wipe my feet on Edom
    and shout in triumph over Philistia."

Who will bring me into the fortified city?
    Who will bring me victory over Edom?
Have you rejected us, O God?
    Will you no longer march with our armies?
Oh, please help us against our enemies,
    for all human help is useless.
With God's help we will do mighty things,
    for he will trample down our foes.

Reflection

"Be exalted, O God!" Psalm 108 is a psalm of intentionality. The psalmist doesn't simply praise God, but instead resolves to deliberately exalt the Most High God.

The psalmist is also intentional about praising God in public. This is key. The psalmist lives a life that boldly proclaims the goodness of the Lord. Sometimes we get so caught up in our individual piety that no one else hears us when we praise God. But praise is communal! When we honor God for who God has been to us, it is also a time to honor who God has been to our communities, to our families, to our organizations, and more.

Psalm 108 tells us to make a big deal over who God is and what God has done! I want to encourage you to be bold about how you praise God today. Let somebody encounter you speaking well of God. This intimate time of reflection is wonderful, but are you sharing it? Are you telling others about how great God is? Are you illustrating the ways in which you rely upon God? Let Psalm 108 be our reminder that God deserves boisterous praise. Don't hide your faith. God has been too good for you to hold it in. They used to sing, "Said I wasn't gonna tell nobody but I couldn't keep it to myself what the Lord has done for me!" Go ahead and tell somebody how good God has been to you. Your soul will thank you for it. Praise God among the people, praise God among the nations! Don't keep this good news to yourself!

Devotional

Chance the Rapper famously proclaimed, "I speak to God in public." Likewise, the psalmist enjoins us to praise God from an exuberant heart. On this final day of our devotional journey, go public with your praise!

Email your loved ones, post it on social media, send it to your group chat. In your preferred medium, amplify the goodness of the Lord for all to witness, that your testimony might pique the curiosity of others. When we praise God publicly, we embody a justice imagination. Doing this work reminds the world that our highest praise isn't reserved for ourselves. It definitely isn't reserved for our governments or capitalist economics. Our Halleujah, instead, goes to a Creator who supplies all that we need to survive and thrive as human beings. When our work springs from that starting point of faith, it reveals every attempt to restrict access for God's material abundance to the few, rather than the many, as a betrayal of the divine intent for the world.

But when we praise the God of all Black lives, in whom we find the world's salvation, we praise the One who calls us all, without exclusion, to freedom and abundant life. In Christ's name, by the power of the Spirit, we give God our praise and offer up the justice work to which we have committed our labor, intelligence, our talent, our very lives. Amen.

Questions for the Day

- How can you remind your soul to intentionally experience each day? What practices do you have to awaken your body each day?
- What commitments have you made to yourself to fully experience each day of your life?
- What does it look like to live a life of loving, savoring, and serving God?

PRACTICING PSALMS FOR BLACK LIVES: A COMMUNITY AND CONGREGATIONAL STUDY GUIDE

The Psalms are meant to be sung, chanted, spoken, and above all, embodied and practiced in our lived experience. To aid your congregation or community in embodying the Psalms, we have prepared a month-long study guide with prompts, exercises, and models for walking through *Psalms for Black Lives*.

This resource is designed to be used on a weekly basis, but can also be adapted for a different schedule in accordance with your desired goals. If the first part of the devotional is meant to make room for the Psalms in the hearts and minds of Black diasporic people, then this part is meant to impact our practices so that the work of our collective hands contributes to the undoing of structural racism, to an equitable economy for all God's creation, and to an embodied spirituality that claims God's yes in our beautiful, dark skin.

Week 1: Direct Service and Psalms for Black Lives

This week, we encourage you to pair each daily reflection with an act of direct service to meet the needs of your community. Cultivating a justice imagination begins with local, coordinated acts of service. These acts of service build relationships, help us understand the complexities of the needs in the area, and establish the foundations for the work of systemic change that a justice imagination inspires. This service could take the form of organizing a job and resource fair to connect individuals with employment opportunities and local government agencies that can address their immediate needs. It might also look like partnering with local congregations or nonprofit organizations to put together a food or clothing drive.

Whatever you decide, the most important thing is to engage your community or congregation as deeply as possible, encourage the use of the devotional on a daily basis, and make the connection between the two.

Monday, Day 1

Convene the congregation or community to identify direct service opportunities in your area. Marian Wright Edelman, the esteemed founder of the Children's Defense Fund, proclaimed that "service is the rent we pay for living." Her framework for service underscores the importance of servant leadership and recognizing that we exist not to be served, but to serve.

Consider setting aside time to read today's reflection and then identify an area where your congregation or community can meaningfully and directly address the needs of your neighbors.

Tuesday, Day 2

Having identified direct service opportunities, build consensus on which opportunities to prioritize. Psalm 133:1 articulates the beauty and goodness of being in one accord rejoicing, "How very good and pleasant it is when kindred live together in unity!" Before embarking on volunteer initiatives, it's important to ensure that everyone has bought into the plan. The character of this consensus also matters, particularly alignment on the inherent value of every human being. Opportunities to serve should be seen by all as encounters between equals, regardless of distinctions in social status that may exist between those who serve and those who are served.

Wednesday and Thursday, Day 3 and Day 4

Dedicate the next two days to engaging in direct service in your community. Spend two days inviting your community to do the work of meeting the immediate needs and issues of individuals and institutions in your community. Helping to provide volunteer income tax assistance, registering voters, and investing sweat equity to repair a dilapidated apartment not only cultivate our communities; such acts also cultivate our spirits while building our justice imagination.

Friday, Day 5

Debrief with your community after your week of direct service. Use an action-reflection model to promote a complex understanding of the root causes that gave rise to the need for direct service in the first place. Orchestrating a canned food drive is a great first step, but it must eventually evolve into questioning why food drives are needed in certain communities but not others. This is your opportunity to explore questions like why food drives too often substitute for and supplant a widespread commitment to eradicating hunger and food insecurity in all neighborhoods, particularly the neighborhoods of Black, Latinx, and Indigenous people.

Week 2: Community Development and Psalms for Black Lives

Direct service is essential, but not enough to build a justice imagination. To build on the foundation of direct service, this week we invite you to pair your daily engagement of the Psalms with an act of community development. Direct service opportunities usually entail individually coordinated acts of volunteering that meet immediate needs. By contrast, community development generally involves an institutional approach to meeting both immediate *and* long-term needs. This undertaking builds a justice imagination by helping us envision organizational responses—not just personal ones—to injustice and unmet needs.

Monday, Day 1

Supporting programs that already work to address the needs of individuals and neighborhoods in targeted ways helps to curate a justice imagination. The first step toward supporting these programs is to identify them. Survey the community development happening already within your congregation or your community. Is your congregation or community already doing work that could benefit from an annual review? If they are, what adjustments can be made to accentuate what works and stop what doesn't?

For example, where are foreclosure prevention and rental assistance programs being provided? What steps is your city, state, or county level government doing to provide consumer protection, preventative health, and other basic services?

Start this week off by pairing your engagement of the Psalms with an internal and external diagnosis of community development programs happening in your area.

Tuesday, Day 2

Determine where you can add most value. After surveying community development initiatives in your area, pray and conduct research about the unique impact that your congregation or institution can help provide. Part of activating a justice imagination is ensuring that our involvement makes a tangible difference in the lives of people and their environments, rather than being a matter of perfunctory engagement. As you work through today's psalm and reflection, consider where you can make the most change in your community.

Wednesday, Day 3

Organize an all-in community development initiative across two days. Building out a justice imagination is a "we" proposition, not an "I" proposition. By galvanizing a community development initiative like this, you can create an identity of collective service and a spirit of teamwork in your congregation or institution. Orchestrating an event of this sort could look like connecting individuals and families to first-time homebuyer programs, volunteering at a nearby community development corporation, or helping a local worker co-op access local government support for public contracting opportunities.

Thursday, Day 4

Continue engagement in community development. Today marks the culmination of your community or congregation's two-day initiative to support community development work in your area. As you embark on today's work, be sure to review the breadth of participation in your initiative. Strive to extend an opportunity for service and engagement to everyone within your context. This will heighten the odds that everyone, rather than a select few, has the chance to cultivate a justice imagination that emerges from a collective and personal encounter with God through the Psalms.

Friday, Day 5

Reflect on your participation in community development. As you near the conclusion of your community development week, create a communal space to make sense of your experiences. How do direct service and community development complement one another? What are the relative strengths and weaknesses of each approach? In the language of Psalm 85:10, in what respects do community service and community development anticipate a time where "righteousness and peace will kiss each other"—that is, where everyone has what is due to them (righteousness) and it has been obtained through nonviolent, harmonious means (peace)?

Week 3: Direct Action, Advocacy, and Psalms for Black Lives

Direct action and advocacy are the next steps for a community or congregation seeking to cultivate a justice imagination. Direct action and advocacy, especially when targeting the public sector, differs from community development and direct service by seeking to change systems rather than pursuing change through operating programs and mobilizing volunteers. By conducting direct action, organizing public policy advocacy activities, and sitting with a psalm of devotion each day this week, we help advance God's intentions of working "justice for all who are oppressed" (Psalm 103:6).

Monday, Day 1

Research the direct action and advocacy work taking place in your community. Uncovering direct action and advocacy opportunities provides an accessible pathway for cultivating a justice imagination that seeks to not only meet immediate needs but to change the systems that produce those needs in the first place. Good direct action and advocacy seeks to end hunger, not just alleviate it for a moment. It seeks to eradicate homelessness, not simply mitigate it. As you begin this week of encounters with *Psalms for Black Lives*, think of how to pursue both quality and large-scale responses as you identify direct action and advocacy opportunities for your community to engage.

Tuesday, Day 2

Discuss the opportunities available and decide which direct actions or advocacy efforts your congregation or community will support. Arrange a time and place to collectively talk through the direct actions and advocacy efforts your community or congregation will prioritize. Having public conversations that precede and help determine advocacy priorities is a great way to both ensure buy-in and to make certain that your congregation or community is a space of genuine belonging that values the charge from Isaiah 1:18 to "let us argue it out." Additionally, public discussion helps the entire congregation or community, not just the pastors or senior leaders, embody a justice imagination.

Wednesday, Day 3

Engage in direct action and advocacy across the next two days. Rev. Dr. Martin Luther King Jr. once observed that, "Human progress is neither automatic nor inevitable . . . Every step toward the goal of justice requires sacrifice, suffering, and struggle; the tireless exertions and passionate concern of dedicated individuals." In the spirit of Dr. King, embark upon your two-day advocacy summit with the assurance that an activated justice imagination is a refusal to let the chips fall where they may. Instead of fatalism, it is an insistence that God's will for justice be done on earth as in heaven. It is also an insistence that this will for justice be approximated in our systems and not confined to disconnected individual efforts or isolated programs.

Thursday, Day 4

Continue engaging in direct action and advocacy. As you continue to advocate for systemic change through public policy advocacy and direct action, elevate the importance of steadfast action and trust in God's involvement for the survival of all Black lives. As Psalm 90 maintains, God is our dwelling place throughout all generations. God is our first and deepest source of motivation as we seek to establish customs, practices, and legal frameworks that disrupt inter-generational poverty, racial disparities, and other kinds of oppression besieging God's people.

Friday, Day 5

Reflect on the process and outcomes of direct action and advocacy in light of the Psalms. Having conducted a week of advocacy and direct action, set aside today to see the big picture. How does God's call toward justice and liberation for all Black lives connect us to service, community development, and advocacy? How do the Psalms draw a link between spirituality that addresses both immediate needs and long-term needs, while also striving to remove the root causes of community needs? When addressing questions like these, be sure to create space for individual reflection and small-group conversation. A justice imagination becomes deeper when the entire church or community can reflect together and together encounter the God of the Psalms, who executes justice for the oppressed and gives food to the hungry (Psalm 146:7).

Week 4: Regional Planning and Psalms for Black Lives

Regional and community planning is the last dimension of practicing a justice imagination. Regional planning, for instance, focuses on zoning decisions about which parts of our land will be used for housing, as well as which parts will be used for parks, office towers, and industrial use. Using our justice imagination means adopting a community design mindset as we steward these resources of God's creation through this democratic process, rather than taking our natural or built environment as a fixed matter. Regional planning asks questions like, "What if we built state-of-the-art public housing for lower-income families?" and "What if we distributed commercial waste facilities equitably across our communities?"

This week, pair your daily psalms and devotionals with planning activities that influence questions about where and how schools are built, as well as questions that shape how public investment for economic development occurs in your community. By linking the Psalms to local and regional planning, we partner with the Lord in shaping the future of our communities, instead of accepting unjust social conditions as our unchangeable fate.

Monday, Day 1

Research how and when regional planning takes place in your community. Regional planning uses our justice imagination by proactively seeking to craft the distribution of assets, land, employment opportunities, cultural programming, and money to facilitate human thriving and healthy ecosystems.

Where service, community development, and advocacy are largely reactive, regional planning is a future-oriented exercise of design, projection, and a desire to craft environments that are people-first, not property-centered. Work with your church or community to identify opportunities to engage in regional planning in your community. This could include anything from planning commission meetings on zoning to economic development authority hearings on how and where to distribute public property and tax incentives.

Tuesday, Day 2

Determine how your congregation or community will engage in regional planning. After unearthing possible opportunities for your church or community to engage in local and regional planning activities, select the areas where you will engage. In making your institutional choices, walk through the Psalms as a devotional resource and think about how and when you will offer the option to advance an equity-centered vision of regional planning.

Wednesday, Day 3

Engage or prepare to engage in regional planning activities that impact your community. Planning, fundamentally, is an expression of design. By engaging in regional planning, we exercise power by abolishing certain designs within our area *and* redesigning how services, programs, and systems will operate within our community. As you move through the Psalms, keep in mind the holiness of articulating a comprehensive vision that forges a different architecture of justice, one that differs profoundly from the world we currently inhabit. Imagine a world where our economy is green rather than grey; where multiple standards of beauty exist, rather than only one dominant, often white, ideal; where social wealth is used for the common good instead of being privatized for the benefit of a relatively small group.

Thursday, Day 4

Continue engaging and preparing for regional planning activities in your community. As your congregation or community carries out your second day of regional planning activities, think through how to inclusively create engagement opportunities that can meet the full range of lived experiences in your community. For instance, are regional planning activities accessible to multi-language learners for whom English isn't their first language, or for individuals whose jobs may not allow discretion over their work schedule? Deliberately crafting activities that maximize entry points across a variety of lived experiences helps form a spacious justice imagination whose parameters are as wide and varied as the churches and communities that we serve.

Friday, Day 5

Reflect on the process and outcomes of regional planning activities in light of the Psalms. As your congregational and community study concludes for this week, as well as for the month, take the opportunity to synthesize the lessons you've learned from living out the Psalms by engaging in direct service, community development, advocacy, and regional planning. Each of these four activities helps organize our world based on God's justice. In the words of Psalm 24:1, we recognize that, "The earth is the LORD's and all that is in it, the world, and those who live in it."

How can each member of your community advance the moral imperative of planning for a world filled with distributive and restorative justice, a world with a rightly ordered society where all Black lives, and all of God's creation, can access what they inherently deserve and deeply need to experience that abundant life that Christ intends for us? Where might the Spirit be calling you to make personal and institutional changes? Whose voices need to be heard more clearly, more consistently? What have you been developing a justice imagination to achieve? What is God urging you to create so that this outcome will come to be?

Sit with these questions, answer them as best you can, and watch how God's presence continues to permeate and consecrate your efforts toward a deeper commitment to the intertwined works of love and justice.

ACKNOWLEDGMENTS

Writing a book, as is often acknowledged, is an inherently communal process. We are grateful for the deep partnership and collaborative engagement of the Upper Room Books family. Joanna, Ben, Lisa, Terrell, Dylan, and the entire team at Upper Room Books have made this process a deeply enjoyable, stretching, and meaningful one. Your belief in this devotional and what it could be in the world has been a blessing to us, and we pray, a blessing to the readers.

We would also like to acknowledge Chelsea for her careful ministry of administration, operations, and strategy. Chelsea swooped in at the time that we needed her the most. As a published writer herself and a founding member of Double Love, her commitment to keeping us accountable to our deadlines and deliverables was absolutely invaluable. Follow her work. She writes under the name C. Sylviolet Smith.

Recommended by
The Academy
for spiritual Formation®
THE UPPER ROOM

For those who hunger for deep spiritual experience . . .

The Academy for Spiritual Formation® is an experience of disciplined Christian community emphasizing holistic spirituality—nurturing body, mind, and spirit. The program, a ministry of The Upper Room®, is ecumenical in nature and meant for all those who hunger for a deeper relationship with God, including both lay and clergy persons. Each Academy fosters spiritual rhythms—of study and prayer, silence and liturgy, solitude and relationship, rest and play.

With offerings of both Two-Year and Five-Day models, Academy participants rediscover Christianity's rich spiritual heritage through worship, learning, and fellowship. During the Two-Year Academy, pilgrims gather at a retreat center for five days every three months over the course of two years (a total of 40 days), and the Five-Day Academy is a modified version of the Two-Year experience, inviting pilgrims to gather for five days of spiritual learning and worship. The Academy's commitment to an authentic spirituality promotes balance, inner and outer peace, holy living and justice living—God's shalom.

Faculty trained in the wide breadth of Christian spirituality and practice provide content and guidance at each session of The Academy. Academy faculty presenters come from seminaries, monasteries, spiritual direction ministries, and pastoral ministries or other settings and are from a variety of traditions.

The ACADEMY RECOMMENDS program seeks to highlight content that aligns with the Academy's mission to create transformative space for people to connect with God, self, others, and creation for the sake of the world.

Learn more by visiting academy.upperroom.org.

CPSIA information can be obtained
at www.ICGtesting.com
Printed in the USA
JSHW050141080822
29014JS00006B/19

9 780835 820073